▶▶▶ Rave Reviews ◀◀◀

"...lots of authentic, historical pictures. ...a wonderful job of putting this book together.

...you will actually feel the joy, anguish and determination of the brave people who settled this land...

"The Golden Corridor" is beautifully organized...

...**this is the one book you need to have.** You will spend hours reading the writings of those who were here and delight in the restored pictures of that era."

Mountain Democrat, Placerville

"Fans of old photographs...will love "The Golden Corridor." The book is filled with amazing black and white photos that bring early Northern California to life.

Sidebars on each page give fascinating quotes from diaries, journals and newspapers, as well as anecdotes.

I am a lifelong resident of Northern California, and I learned from this book... "The Golden Corridor" is well worth checking out."

The Union, Nevada County

...a captivating study of 19th century people who helped shape the times.

Sacramento Bee

"... this amazing collection of firsthand testimony... Sidebars offer amusing quick vignettes from the era! **Enthusiastically recommended reading...**

Midwest Book Reviews

"...**educational and entertaining.** Profusely illustrated..."
Auburn Journal

[The Golden Corridor]...
...is the one book you need to have. You will spend hours reading the writings of those who were here and delight in the restored pictures of that era."

Mountain Democrat

THE
GOLDEN CORRIDOR

19th Century Northern California from San Francisco to Lake Tahoe

Including Sacramento, Folsom, Placerville, Auburn, Colfax, Truckee and smaller communities in between.

Written and photographed by the people who lived and made Northern California's history.

Acknowledgements

This book is dedicated to the thousands of pioneers who wrote California's history, the early photographers who captured the scenes and the hundreds of historians who have preserved it over the years.

This work would not have been possible without the help of dozens of libraries, librarians and archivists including:

The California State Library

The Folsom Historical Society

The Library of Congress

Sacramento Archives and Museum Collection Center (SAMCC)

Bancroft Library

Steve Crandell

As we searched the vast libraries for the appropriate photographs, we found many of the same photos in different archives. The attributions are based on the archive from which we actually obtained the image. Any corrections or suggestions are welcome. Our apologies for any real or perceived errors.

The GOLDEN CORRIDOR

Written by:
California pioneers and 19th Century historians.

Researched and compiled by
Jody & Ric Hornor
Photo restoration by
Ric Hornor & Steve Crandell

Published by:

Century Books

An Imprint of Electric Canvas™
1001 Art Road
Pilot Hill, CA 95664
916.933.4490

www.19thCentury.us

Library of Congress, Lawrence & Houseworth Collection

A Mormon wagon train rests for the night near Lake Tahoe, early 1860s.

Introduction

Relive the hopes and dreams of California's early settlers. Read the actual words of dozens of pioneers who recorded their thoughts and deeds in journals, books and letters home.

See nearly 200 sights they saw through 19th Century photographs.

If you live in Northern California you'll recognize many of the places and events that occurred. If you're a tourist in Northern California, you'll find the book follows the travel routes you'll take while sightseeing -- the same routes that cost the lives of hundreds of early pioneer settlers. After a brief overview of the events that lead up to the Gold Rush, you'll travel from San Francisco via Sacramento and then on to Lake Tahoe via Highway 50. You'll visit Folsom, Placerville and the mountain communities of the high Sierras. You'll return over Donner Pass and down I-80 with visits in Truckee, Grass Valley, Nevada City, Auburn and numerous smaller communities along the way. You'll relive history along the entire route. You can visit the historic towns through the 19th century photos and words captured in this book, or better yet, make a real stop and visit their museums and historical sites while you're there.

Feel the joy, anguish and determination of the brave people who settled this land. Enjoy their humor, admire their flair.

Culled down from approximately 5,000 pages of detailed information recorded in the 19th century, *The Golden Corridor* will give you a glimpse of the many monumental accomplishments, brave souls and exciting times that made California what it is today. You'll find the key points of history delivered in the colorful language of the time. Each individual contributor's writing style has its own character.

Words were spelled differently in those days. Punctuation and sentence structure were often different as well. They're challenging to read, but worth the effort.

Political correctness had not yet been invented when the original texts were written. As degrading as some of the terms are, they do reflect history. And keep in mind that history, as it was recorded in the 19th Century, was often done subjectively. Many of the county history books were paid for by the support of the people whose lives were chronicled within them. Thus the poor, or not so vain, may have been omitted unless they were truly newsworthy.

Also, as you read from chapter to chapter, you'll find very different formats and writing styles. That's because the main body of text in each chapter comes from different sources. The Annals of San Francisco, for instance, was written in a journal format with dated entries. Later that same book provides undated "overviews" of various aspects of San Francisco life. The works quoted in other portions of this book were written very differently as you'll see. Just remember, the goal is to preserve these styles for you to enjoy. So, we have specifically done nothing that will make the chapters consistent in their presentation, punctuation, spelling or format as it would eliminate each contributor's personal style and flavor in doing so.

The 176 photographs give you a great look at the times, but keep in mind that, even though photography was around for many years prior to the Gold Rush, there was little photographic equipment in California until about 1850 and few photos were taken before the early 1860s. *The Golden Corridor* gives you a rare look at a couple of the "oldest known" photos of various regions in *The Golden Corridor's* geographic coverage area. There are numerous photos from the Lawrence & Houseworth collection, first published in 1866. That collection is so vast, however, it's probably safe to assume the photos were taken throughout the 1860s.

Many of these original photographs are so damaged that it's nearly impossible to see the detail in them. Hundreds of hours of restoration have gone into the photographs used in *The Golden Corridor*. Many of the original photos are in the public domain and available through the organizations noted with each image. Some are from private collections and copyrighted. In all cases the restoration work is copyrighted. Take a look at the two examples below, and the final version on the noted pages to see for yourself the dramatic difference restoration makes.

See page 101

See page 34

For the purpose of historical accuracy, it's important to note that modern historians have now concluded that January 24th (not the 19th), 1848 is the correct date of gold discovery. According to experts at the Marshall Gold Discovery State Historic Park, in Coloma, California, "Marshall swore 'till the day he died that January 19th, 1848 was the day he discovered gold." But, historians have compared all the journals of the early settlers and have concluded that January 24th is the correct gold discovery date. Please note that all the references in the early history books state "January 19, 1848." Since this work is drawn precisely from those early works, the date is shown as they recorded it, even though it has since been proven inaccurate.

So have fun wandering through 19th Century California. Get a taste of its rich history. And, if this book has whet your appetite for more, use the bibliography from *The Golden Corridor* as a guide, find yourself a library with a good California reference section, and have fun with your studies!

Side Bar Legend

Most of the side bars provide new information that is not contained in the main body of text. The nature of the information is denoted by the following icons:

Text from personal letters will appear in this script font with the quill pen.

Stories about crime will appear with the hangman's noose in this font.

Quotes from diaries or journals will appear with this image of President Taft's personal journal.

Call outs, text that appears in the main body of content, highlighted for emphasis, appears with this magnifying glass.

You'll also occasionally find direct quotes from old newspaper articles which are simply quoted and sourced.

Table of Contents

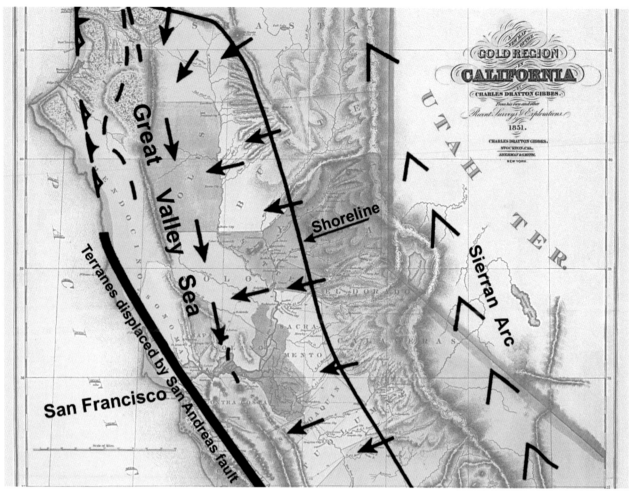

Preface: The Gold Rush - A Saga 500 Million Years In the Making

IN THE LATE Paleozoic Era (543 to 248 Million Years Ago), much of Northern California was covered by an inland sea. The land slowly rose, while the sea receded for millions of years before the first volcanic eruptions. It is believed that a pre-Sierran mountain range existed around 150 millions years ago with elevations as high as 15,000 feet. Through the process of erosion, that range was slowly reduced to rolling hills over the next 80 million years allowing layer upon layer of sedimentary, volcanic and metamorphic rock to be stripped off and carried west to the valley below. Uplift of the present Sierra Nevada is believed to have started about 10 million years ago.

Gold-bearing deposits were laid down over the millennia. They were exposed in a series of volcanism, uplifting, faulting, and erosion episodes that took place over the last 150 million

...a pre-Sierran mountain range existed around 150 millions years ago with elevations as high as 15,000 feet.

years. Mineralized quartz veins appeared, formed by the filling and enlargement of cracks in the rock by siliceous materials.

During the Cretaceous period, 60-95 million years ago, a sea once again covered much of Northern California and erosion removed several miles of deposit from the tops of the Sierra, exposing the gold-bearing veins. Over the next 25 million years the gold was released from the rocks and veins, forming deposits of white quartz gravel and placer gold, which, 25 million years hence were found in virtually every streambed in the Mother Lode.

During the Tertiary period (65 to 1.8 million years ago) auriferous gravels were covered once again by volcanic lava and mud flows. These ancient river channels came to be known as "dry diggings" during the Gold Rush.

About 10 million years ago, three faults conspired to create a deep valley where Lake Tahoe now sits. An incredible valley with steep canyon walls and a river at its bottom was the first ancient river through the area. After the formation of the great river valley, volcanic activity again shook the Tahoe area. With no way to escape, runoff began to fill in the deep canyon. Over thousands of years, Lake Tahoe slowly filled to a level 700 to 800 feet higher than it is presently.

Twenty thousand years ago early man found his way across the Bering Straits and settled in the vast area we now call California.

Discoveries made during the California Gold Rush (1849-1850s) found a prehistoric mining shaft, 210 feet below the surface in solid rock. A mortar for grinding gold ore was found at a depth of 300 feet in a mining tunnel. A human skull was also found at a depth of 130 feet under five beds of lava and tufa. Bones of camels, rhinoceroses, hippopotamuses, horses, and other animals were also found in California. The findings are almost always in gold-bearing rock or gravel.

Prior to its destruction by quarrying operations, the Hawver Cave near Cool (Highway 49, El Dorado County) was known to paleontologists as a storehouse of Pleistocene fossils. Between 1908 and 1910, J.C. Hawver exhumed a quantity of human bones at the lower end of the main shaft, from a loose mass of earth and rock. Artifacts recovered from the cave have been dated to 2,500 years ago.

Over 25 million years the gold was released from the rocks and veins, forming deposits of white quartz gravel and placer gold, which 25 million years hence were found in virtually every streambed in the Mother Lode.

1860s, Emigrant Wagon Train Crossing the Sierra Nevada Mountains at Strawberry Valley (Highway 50).

Chapter 1: European Explorers and The First Discovery of Gold

The very first knowledge of precious metals was the discovery of silver at Avizal, in Monterey county, in 1802. The following letter [from Thomas Sprague] is an important document, showing that Jedediah S. Smith was not only the first white man to come overland to California, but that to him is due the first discovery of gold in California:

Jedediah S. Smith was not only the first white man to come overland to California, but that to him is due the first discovery of gold in California.

Emigrants at Smith Flat, 1848

"Smith pushed on down Mary's river, and being of an adventuresome nature, when he found his road closed by high mountains, determined to see what kind of a country there was on the other side."

"GENOA, CARSON VALLEY," September 18th, 1860. "EDMOND RANDOLPH, ESQ., S. F.:

"FRIEND RANDOLPH — I have known of the J. S. Smith you mentioned, by reputation, for many years. He was the first white man that ever went overland from the Atlantic States to California. He was the chief trader in the employ of the American Fur Company. At the rendezvous of the company on Green river, near the South Pass, in 1825, Smith was directed to take charge of a party of some forty men (trappers) and penetrate the country west of Salt Lake. He discovered what is now known as Humboldt river. He called it Mary's river, from his Indian wife, Mary.

"Smith pushed on down Mary's river, and being of an adventuresome nature, when he found his road closed by high mountains, determined to see what kind of a country there was on the other side.

"The gold that he brought with him, together with his description of the country, and the large amount of furs, pleased the agent of the American Fur Company so well that he directed Smith again to make the same trip, with special instructions to take the gold fields on his return and thoroughly prospect them. The trip was successful until they arrived in the vicinity of the gold mines, east of the mountains, where, in a battle with the Indians, Smith and nearly all his men were killed. A few of the party escaped and reached the encampment on Green river.

This defeat damped the ardor of the company so much that they never looked any more for the gold mines."

"In 1843, Sutter's fort was visited by a young Swedish scholar, Dr. Santels, known as the "King's Orphan," on account of having been educated at a government institution of Sweden, which education bore with others the requirement of traveling in foreign lands. After having finished his examination trip through the country this gentleman wrote in 1843:

"The Californias are rich in minerals; gold, silver, lead, oxide of iron, manganese and copper ore are met with throughout the country, the precious metals being the most abundant."

All these many discoveries and statements of the existence of precious metals, however had not effect enough to excite a single soul. This is what was reserved to the final discovery of placer gold in the mill-race at Coloma, on January 19, 1848, by James W. Marshall, which, spreading like an epidemic disease, produced a new one—the gold fever— that soon revolutionized the whole civilized world; and the name of California heretofore almost unknown, found its way to the ear of almost every person of culture in the old as well as in the new world.

INDIAN GUIDES HELP FREEMONT CROSS THE SIERRAS

John C. Fremont, then Brevet Captain of Topographical Engineers passed south on the east side of the Sierra Nevada. On the evening of January 28, 1844, the party of twenty-five men passed the mountain range dividing the Carson river from the basin of Lake Tahoe, and from here we may follow the verbal quotation of the report:

All these many discoveries and statements of the existence of precious metals, however had not effect enough to excite a single soul...

Map of the Gold Region, 1860

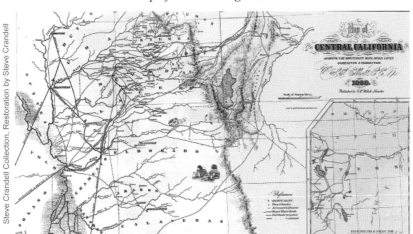

Steve Crandell Collection, Restoration by Steve Crandell

Steve Crandell Collection, Restoration by Steve Crandell

Gold fever brought thousands of miners from around the world as seen in this 1850 photograph.

"The gold fever that soon revolutionized the whole civilized world; and the name of California, heretofore almost unknown, found its way to the ear of almost every person of culture in the old as well as in the new world."

"Jan. 28. — To-day we went through the pass with all the camp, and, after a hard day's journey of twelve miles, encamped on a high point where the snow had been blown off, and the exposed grass afforded a scanty pasture for the animals. Snow and broken country together made our traveling difficult; we were often compelled to make large circuits, and ascend the highest and most exposed ridges.

During the day a few Indians were seen circling around us on snow shoes, and skimming along like birds; but we could not bring them within speaking distance. They seem to have no idea of the power of firearms, and think themselves perfectly safe beyond arm's length.

To-night we did not succeed in getting the howitzer into camp. This was the most laborious day we had yet passed through, the steep ascent and deep snow exhausting both men and animals.

We followed a trail down a hollow where the Indians had descended, the snow being so deep that we never came near the ground; but this only made our descent so much easier, and, when we reached a little affluent to the river at the bottom, we suddenly found ourselves in the presence of eight or ten Indians. Our friendly demeanor reconciled them, and when we got near enough they immediately stretched out to us handfuls of pine nuts, which seemed an exercise of hospitality. The lower parts of these mountains were covered with the nut-pine. Several Indians appeared on the hillside, reconnoitering the camp, and were induced to come in. Others came in during the afternoon, and in the evening we held a council. We explained to the Indians that we were endeavoring to find a passage across the mountains into the country of the whites, and told them that we wished them to bring us a guide, to whom we would give presents of scarlet cloth and other articles, which were shown to them. They looked at the reward we offered, and conferred with each other, but pointed to the snow in the mountains, and drew their hands across their necks and raised them above their heads, to show the depth. They made signs that we must go to the southward, over a pass through a lower range, which they pointed out. There, they said, at the end of one day's travel, we would find people who lived near a pass in the great mountain, and to that point they engaged to furnish a guide.

The Indians brought in during the evening an abundant supply of pine-nuts, for which we traded with them. When roasted, their pleasant flavor made them an agreeable addition to our now scanty store of provisions, which were reduced to a very low ebb. Our principal stock was in peas, which contained

At the time of European contact, the native peoples living in the Tahoe area included the Washoe Indians, seen here in the mid-1800s.

Library of Congress, Lawrence & Housewerth Collection

Another class of men from the Rocky Mountains were in the habit of making their way by the Mojave Desert south of the Sierra Nevada into California to steal horses, sometimes driving off four or five hundred at a time.

General John Bidwell, 1841

Outbreaks of violence followed throughout the Mother Lode. Far worse, however, was the spread of the white man's diseases, such as smallpox, typhus, pneumonia, and venereal disease, from which the natives had no immunity. This is a scene in a Digger Indian Camp in the mid-1800s.

My situation, alone among strange Indians killing our poor horses, was by no means comfortable.

They were known as the Horse Thief Indians, and lived chiefly on horse flesh.

A day or two later we came to a place where there was a great quantity of horse bones. They were of course horses that the Indians had driven in there and slaughtered. A few miles away we came to a village; the Indians had fled, but we found the horses killed and some of the meat roasting on a fire.

General John Bidwell, 1841

scarcely any nutriment. We had still a little flour left, some coffee, and a quantity of sugar, which I reserved as a defense against starvation. The Indians informed us that in a certain season they have fish in their waters which we supposed to be salmon-trout; for the remainder of the year they live on pine-nuts, which form their great winter subsistence, a portion being always at hand, shut up in the natural storehouse of the cones. They were presented to us as a whole people, living upon this simple vegetable.

January 30th — Our guide, who was a young man, joined us this morning, and leaving our encampment late in the day, we descended the river which immediately opened out into a broad valley, furnishing good traveling ground. In a short distance we passed the village, a collection of straw huts; and a few miles below the guide pointed out the place where the whites had camped before entering the mountains. With our late start we made but ten miles, and encamped on the low river bottom, where there was no snow but a great deal of ice, and we cut piles of long grass to lay under our blankets, and fires were made of the large dry willows. The river here took a northeasterly direction, on the left, was a gap where we were to pass the next day.

January 31— We took our way over a gently rising ground, the dividing ridge being tolerably low, and traveling easily along with a broad train, in twelve or fourteen miles reached the upper part of the pass, when it began to snow thickly, with very cold weather. The Indians had only the usual scanty covering, and appeared to suffer greatly from cold. All left us except our guide. Half hidden by the storm, the mountains looked dreary; and as night began to approach the guide began to show great reluctance to go forward. I placed him between two rifles, for the way began to be difficult. Traveling a little farther we struck a ravine which the Indian said would conduct us to the river; and as the poor fellow suffered greatly, shivering in the snow which fell upon his naked skin, I would not detain him any longer, and he ran off to the mountain. He had kept the blue and scarlet cloth I had given him tightly rolled up, preferring rather to endure the cold than to get them wet. We had made a forced march of twenty-six miles, and three mules had given out on the road; we have now sixty-seven animals in the band.

As gold deposits decreased, white miners became increasingly hostile to Indian miners, viewing them as competition. The first conflict occurred when a party of Oregon miners came upon a rancheria of Southern Maidu and raped several of the Maidu women. When several Indians attempted to interfere, they were shot by the miners. Shortly afterward, a group of five Oregonians were attacked by a party of Indians at a spot on the Middle Fork of the American River, later known as Murderer's Bar.

With a large present of goods, we prevailed upon this young man to be our guide, and he acquired among us the name of Melo— a word signifying friend, which they used very frequently. We gave him skins to make a new pair of moccasins, he being nearly barefooted, and to enable him to perform his undertaking with us.

By the mid-1850's the surviving native population had become dependent upon the goods they received from the whites. A system of exchange developed where native peoples traded their labor, beads and foodstuffs. This 1904 photo is a Maidu woman living on the Cosumnes River in El Dorado County.

Crossing the river on the ice, and leaving it immediately, we commenced the ascent of the mountain along the valley of a tributary stream. The people were unusually silent, for every man knew that our enterprise was hazardous, and the issue doubtful.

We gathered together a few of the most intelligent of the Indians—that had come into camp nearly naked—and held this evening an interesting council. I explained to them my intentions. I told them that we had come from a very far country, having been traveling now nearly a year, and that we were desirous simply to go across the mountain into the country of the other whites. There were two who appeared particularly intelligent—one, somewhat old man. He told me that before the snows fell, it was six sleeps to the place where the whites lived, but that now it was impossible to cross the mountains on account of the deep snow; and showing us, that it was over our heads, he urged us strongly to follow the course of the river, which, he said, would conduct us to a lake in which there were many large fish. Here, he said, is a young man who has seen the whites with his own eyes; and he swore first by the sky, and then by the ground, that what he said was true. With a large present of goods, we prevailed upon this young man to be our guide, and he acquired among us the name of Melo— a word signifying friend. We gave him skins to make a new pair of moccasins, he being nearly barefooted, and to enable him to perform his undertaking with us. The Indians remained in the camp during the night, and we kept the guide and two others to sleep in the lodge with us—Carson laying across the door, and having made them comprehend the use of our fire-arms.

February 1. — In the morning I acquainted the men with my decision. I reminded them of the beautiful valley of the Sacramento river, with which they were familiar from the description of Carson [Kit Carson], who had been there some fifteen years ago, and who in our late privations had delighted us in speaking of its rich pastures and abounding game. I assured them that from the heights of the mountain before us, we should doubtless see the valley of the Sacramento, and with one effort place ourselves again in the midst of plenty. Our guide was not neglected, extremity of suffering might make him desert, we therefore did the best we could for him. Leggings, moccasins, some articles of clothing and a large green blanket, in addition to the blue and scarlet cloth, were lavished upon him, and to his great and evident contentment. He arrayed himself in all his colors, and clad in green, blue and scarlet, he made a gay looking Indian; and with his various presents, was probably richer and better clothed than any of his tribe had ever been before.

February 2. — It had ceased snowing, and this morning the lower air was clear and frosty; and six or seven thousand feet above, the peaks of the Sierra now and then appeared among the rolling clouds, which were rapidly dispersing before the sun. Crossing the river on the ice, and leaving it immediately, we

"...others still had gone down the Columbia River to Oregon and joined trapping parties in the service of the Hudson Bay Company going from Oregon to California—men who would let their beards grow down to their knees, and wear buckskin garments made and fringed like those of the Indians, and who considered it a compliment to be told "I took ye for an Injin."

General John Bidwell, 1841

Maidu Indian couple shucking acorns, 1902.

Courtesy of the Bancroft Library, University of California, Berkeley

We marvel over the beauty of Eagle Falls at Lake Tahoe today as this man did in the 1860s. But for emigrants coming through the area, it was one more obstacle to conquer on an already horrendously difficult journey.

Our guide was standing by the fire with all his finery on, and seeing him shiver in the cold, I threw on his shoulders one of my blankets. We missed him a few minutes afterwards, and never saw him again; he had deserted us. By observation our latitude was 38°, 42' 26" ; and elevation by the boiling point, 7,400 feet.

commenced the ascent of the mountain along the valley of a tributary stream. The people were unusually silent, for every man knew that our enterprise was hazardous, and the issue doubtful.

February 3.— The snow was so deep in the hollow that we were obliged to travel along the steep hill-sides, and over spurs where the wind and sun had in places lessened the snow, and where the grass, which appeared to be in good quality along the sides of the mountains, was exposed. There being no grass exposed here, the horses were sent back to that we had seen a few miles below. During the day several Indians joined on snow-shoes. These were made of a circular hoop, about a foot in diameter, the interior space being filled with an open network of bark.

February 4. — I went ahead early with two or three men, each with a led horse to break the road.

Toward a pass which the guide indicated here, we attempted in the afternoon to force a road; but after a laborious plunging through two or three hundred yards our best horses gave out, entirely refusing to make any further effort, and we were brought to a stand. The animals generally not having strength enough to bring themselves up without the packs; and all the line of road between this and the springs was strewed with camp-stores and equipage, and horses floundering in the snow. To-night we had no shelter, but we made a large fire around the trunk of one of the huge pines and covering the snow with small boughs, on which to spread our blankets, soon made ourselves comfortable. The night was very bright and clear, though the thermometer was only 10°. A strong wind which sprung up at sundown made it intensely cold, and this was one of the bitterest nights during the journey.

Two Indians joined our party here, and one of them, an old man, immediately began to harangue us, saying that ourselves and animals would perish in the snow; and that if we would go back, he would show us another and better way across the mountains. He spoke in a very loud voice, and there was a singular repetition of phrases and arrangement of words, which rendered his speech striking and not unmusical.

We had now begun to understand some words, and with the aid of signs, easily comprehended the old man's simple idea: "Rock upon rock—rock upon rock; snow upon snow," he said "even if you get over the snow, you will not be able to get down from the mountains." He made us the sign of precipices, and showed us how the feet of the horses would slip. Our Chinook, who comprehended even more readily than ourselves, and be-

Digger (also known as Maidu & Nisenan) Indian Trapper, 1860s.

To-night we had no shelter, but we made a large fire around the trunk of one of the huge pines and covering the snow with small boughs, on which to spread our blankets, soon made ourselves comfortable. The night was very bright and clear, though the thermometer was only 10°.

Falls on the Yuba River near Cisco, mid-1860s.

The meat train did not arrive this evening, and I gave Godey leave to kill our little dog...

lieved our situation hopeless, covered his head with his blanket and began to weep and lament. "I wanted to see the whites, and I don't care to die among them, but here" — and he looked around in the cold night and gloomy forest, and, drawing his blankets over his head, began again to lament.

February 5. — The night had been too cold to sleep, and we were up very early. Our guide was standing by the fire with all his finery on, and seeing him shiver in the cold, I threw on his shoulders one of my blankets. We missed him a few minutes afterwards, and never saw him again; he had deserted us. By observation our latitude was 38°, 42' 26"; and elevation by the boiling point, 7,400 feet.

February 6.— Far below us, dimmed by the distance, was a large snowless valley, bounded on the western side at the distance of about a hundred miles, a low range of mountains, which Carson recognized with delight as the mountains bordering the coast. "There," said he, "is the little mountain, (Mt. Diablo,) it is fifteen years since I saw it; but I am just as sure as if I had seen it yesterday." Between us and this low coast range, then, there was the valley of the Sacramento; and no one who had not accompanied us through the incidents of our life for the last few months, could realize the delight with which at last we looked down upon it.

February 9.— During the night the weather changed, the wind rising to a gale, and commencing to snow before daylight; before morning the trail was covered. We remained quiet in camp all day, in the course of which the weather improved. Four sleighs arrived towards evening, with the bedding of the men. We suffer much from the want of salt, and all the men are becoming weak from insufficient food.

February 10.— The forest here has a noble appearance, and tall cedar is abundant, and here I see for the first time the white pine, of which there are some magnificent trees. The top of a flat ridge near us was bare of snow, and very well sprinkled with bunch-grass, sufficient to pasture the animals for two or three days; and this was to be their main point of support. The glare of the snow, combined with great fatigue, had rendered many of the people nearly blind; but we were fortunate in having some black silk handkerchiefs, which worn as veils, very much relieved the eye.

February 11.— In the evening I received a message from Mr. Fitzpatrick, acquainting me with the utter failure of his attempt to get our mules and horses over the snow,—the half-hidden trail had proved entirely too slight to support them, and

Indian Rancheria in the Sierra Nevada Mountains, mid-1860s.

In the evening I received a message from Mr. Fitzpatrick, acquainting me with the utter failure of his attempt to get our mules and horses over the snow,—the half-hidden trail had proved entirely too slight to support them, and they had broken through, and were plunging about or lying half buried in snow.

Snows impede travel over Johnson Pass in the mid-1860s.

We had again the prospect of a thunder-storm below, and to-night we killed another mule—now our only resource from starvation.

they had broken through, and were plunging about or lying half buried in snow. I wrote him to send the animals immediately back to their old pastures; and after having made mauls and shovels, turn in all the strength of his party to open and beat a road through the snow, strengthening it with boughs and branches of the pines.

February 13. — A party of Indians had passed on snow shoes, who said they were going to the western side of the mountains after fish. This was an indication that the salmon were coming up the streams; and we could hardly restrain our impatience as we thought of them and worked with increased vigor. The meat train did not arrive this evening, and I gave Godey leave to kill our little dog (Tlamath), which he prepared in Indian fashion—scorching off the hair and washing the skin with soap and snow, then cutting it into pieces, which were laid on the snow. Shortly afterward the sleigh arrived with a supply of horse meat, and we had to-night an extraordinary dinner— pea-soup, mule and dog.

February 16.—We had succeeded in getting our animals safely to the first grassy hill, and this morning I started with

Jacob on a reconnoitering expedition beyond the mountain. Towards sundown we discovered some icy spots in a deep hollow, and descending the mountain we encamped on the headwater of a little creek. I was now perfectly satisfied that we had struck the stream on which Mr. Sutter lived, and, turning about, made a hard push and reached the camp at dark. Here we had the pleasure of finding all the remaining animals, 57 in number, safely arrived at the grassy hill near the camp; and here also we were agreeably surprised with the sight of an abundance of salt.

February 21.—We now considered ourselves victorious over the mountain; having only the descent before us and the valley under our eyes. But this was a case in which the descent was *not* facile. Still deep fields of snow lay between them, and there was a large intervening space of rough looking mountains, through which we had yet to wind our way. Carson roused me this morning with an early fire, and we were all up long before day, in order to pass the snow fields before the sun should render the crust soft. We had the satisfaction to know that at least there were people below. Fires were lit up in the valley just at night, appearing to be in answer to ours; and these signs of life renewed, in some measure, the gayety of the camp.

February 22.—Our breakfast was over long before day. We took advantage of the coolness of the early morning to get over

When we overtook the foremost of the party the next morning we found they had come to a pond of water, and one of them had killed a fat coyote; when I came up it was all eaten except the lights and the windpipe, on which I made my breakfast.

General John Bidwell, 1841

Three men cross the Sierra Nevada on the Donner Trail, early 1860s.

The impact of the Gold Rush was hardest on those tribes living squarely in the center of the gold districts, such as Coloma, Auburn and Placerville. Unable to compete with immigrants, the native people were forced to adapt themselves to the new economic and social order of the mining towns.

Most of the way was through the region now lying between Lathrop and Sacramento. We got out of provisions and were about three days without food. Game was plentiful, but hard to shoot. It was impossible to keep our old flint-lock guns dry, and especially the powder dry in the pans. On the eighth day we came to Sutter's settlement. This was November 28, 1841; the fort had not then been begun. Sutter received us with open arms and in a princely fashion, for he was a man of the most polite address and the most courteous manners, a man who could shine in any society.

General John Bidwell, 1841

the snow, which to-day occurred in very deep banks among the timber; but we searched for the coldest places, and the animals passed successfully with their loads over the hard crust. In the after part of the day we saw before us a handsome grassy ridge point, and making a desperate push over a snowfield ten to fifteen feet deep, we happily succeeded in getting the camp across, and encamped on the ridge after a march of three miles. We had again the prospect of a thunder-storm below, and to-night we killed another mule—now our only resource from starvation.

February 24.—We rose at three in the morning. The sky was clear and pure, with a sharp wind from the northeast, and the thermometer 2° below the freezing point. In the course of the morning we struck a footpath, which we were generally able to keep, and the ground was soft to our animal's feet, being sandy, or covered with mould. Green grass began to make its appearance, and occasionally we passed a hill scatteringly covered with it. Here the roaring torrent has already become a river, and we had descended to an elevation of 3,864 feet.

February 27.—We succeeded in fording the stream, and made a trail by which we crossed the point of the opposite hill, which, on the southern exposure, was prettily covered with green grass, and we halted a mile from our last encampment. Below, the precipices on the river forced us to the heights, which we ascended by a steep spur 2,000 feet high—(Pilot Hill). My favorite horse, Proveau, had become very weak, and was scarcely able to bring himself to the top. Traveling here was good except in crossing the ravines, which were narrow, steep and frequent. We caught a glimpse of a deer, the first animal we had seen, but did not succeed in approaching him. Near nightfall we descended into the steep ravine of a handsome creek 30 feet wide, and I was engaged in getting the horses up the opposite hill when I heard a shout from Carson, who had gone ahead a few hundred yards. "Life yet," said he, "life yet; I have found a hill-side sprinkled with grass enough for the night!" We drove along our horses and encamped at the place about dark, and there was just room enough to make a place for shelter on the edge of the stream.

March 3.—At every step the country improved in beauty. The pines were rapidly disappearing the oaks became the principal trees of the forest. Among these the prevailing tree was the evergreen oak, (which by way of distinction we called the live-oak), and with these occurred frequently a new species of oak bearing a long slender acorn, from an inch to an inch and a half in length, which we now began to see formed the principal vegetable food of the inhabitants of this region.

Sutter was starting a colony in the Sacramento Valley. Before Sutter came the Indians had reigned supreme. I now determined to go to Sutter's. Dr. Marsh said we could make the journey in two days, but it took us eight. Winter had come and meant rain. Streams were out of their banks most of the country was overflowed. There were no roads, merely paths, trodden only by Indians and wild game.

General John Bidwell, 1841

Miner's cabin in the Sierras, 1860s.

Kit Carson — *Born in 1809 in Missouri. Carson used New Mexico as a base for fur-trapping expeditions from about 1828 to 1831. He went as far west as California. Carson was known for his self-restraint and temperate lifestyle. In 1842 John C. Fremont hired Carson as a guide. His service with Fremont was documented in widely-read reports of his expeditions, and he quickly became a national hero.*

We staid here some week or more viewing the sights & wonders of this City of a months existence, composed principally of tents & situated on the east bank of the river, & at the mouth of the American fork, & is I think destined to be the pleasantest & most business City in California.

S. SHUFELT, 1850
Written from
Placerville

March 6.—We continued on our road through the same surpassingly beautiful country, entirely unequalled for the pasturage of stock by anything we had ever seen. Our horses had now become so strong that they we able to carry us, and we traveled rapidly—over four miles an hour, four of us riding every alternate hour. In a few hours we reached a large fork, the northern branch of the river, and equal in size to that which we had descended. Together they formed a beautiful stream, 60 to 100 yards wide; which at first, ignorant of the country through which that river ran, we took to be the Sacramento. Following the tracks of the horses and cattle, in search of people, we discovered a small village of Indians. Some of these had on shirts of civilized manufacture, but were otherwise naked, and we could understand nothing of them; they appeared entirely astonished at seeing us. Shortly afterwards we gave a shout at the appearance, on a little bluff, of a neatly-built *adobe* house, with glass windows. We rode up, but to our disappointment found only Indians. We supposed the place to have been abandoned. We now pressed on more eagerly than ever; the river swept around a large bend to the right; the hills lowered down entirely, and gradually entering a broad valley, we came unexpectedly on a large Indian village, where the people looked clean, and wore cotton shirts and various other articles of dress. They immediately crowded around us, and we had the inexpressible delight to find one who spoke a little indifferent Spanish, but who at first confounded us by saying there were no whites in the country; but just then a well-dressed Indian came up, and made his salutations in very well spoken Spanish. In answer to our inquiries, he informed us that we were upon the Rio de los Americanos, (the river of the Americans,) and that it joined the Sacramento about ten miles below. Never did a name sound more sweetly! We felt ourselves among our countrymen; for the name of American, in these distant parts, is applied to the citizens of the United States. To our eager inquiries he answered: "I am a vaquero (cow-herd) in the service of Captain Sutter, and the people of the rancheria work for him." Our evident satisfaction made him communicative; and he went on to say that Captain Sutter was a very rich man, and always glad to see his country people. In a short distance we came in sight of the fort; and, passing on the way of the house of a settler, on the opposite side we forded the river, and in a few miles were met, a short distance from the fort, by Captain Sutter himself. He gave us a most cordial reception—conducted us immediately to his house, and under his hospitable roof we had a night of rest, enjoyment and refreshment, which none but ourselves could appreciate."

Later expeditions and regular teamster routes were better prepared. Here they're feeding the teams on the Placerville Route in the 1860s.

Library of Congress, Lawrence & Houseworth Collection

My Dear Wife
I have heard of a number of cases where they have been obliged to cut flesh from the animals that have died by the roadside to appease the gnawings of hunger.

E. A. Spooner
Augt 25th 1850

Swift's Station, Carson and Lake Bigler Road - eastern summit of Sierra Nevada Mountains in the 1860s.

After the completion of this slow and painful process of cutting the grain [by hand, most labor provided by Indians], it was piled in a huge mound in the center of a large, round corral. Thereupon three or four hundred wild horses were turned in to thresh it, the Indians whooping and yelling to make them run faster.

General John Bidwell, 1841

Thus far General Fremont's report, to which we may add that he started out with fresh horses and provisions the next morning, to attend to and to relieve the main body of the party, left higher up in the mountains under Mr. Fitzpatrick's command; they met them on the second day out, a few miles below the forks of the American river, and Freemont says: "A more forlorn and pitiable sight than they presented, cannot well be imagined." They were all on foot—each man weak and emaciated, leading a horse or mule as week and emaciated as themselves. They had experienced great difficulty in descending the mountains, made slippery by rains and melting snow, and many horses fell over the precipices and were killed, and with some were lost the packs which they carried. Among these was a mule with the plants which were collected since leaving Fort Hall, along a line of 2,000 miles travel. Out of 67 horses and mules with which the party had commenced crossing the Sierra, only 33 reached the Sacramento valley, and they only in a condition to be led along. None of the men were lost, though a few of them got weak-minded on the last part of the journey, caused from the privations and exposures and overstrained exertions in crossing the mountains.

The Clipper Ship, "Flying Cloud," is one of the most famous ships to make the trip around Cape Horn to deliver adventurers to California. The Flying Cloud was launched April 15, 1851 at the shipyard of Donald McKay, East Boston, for Enoch Train. She made an 89 day record run from New York to San Francisco during the California Gold Rush.

Chapter 2: Gold!

Since the St. Louis newspapers, in 1840, had published the glowing description of California, out of Dr. Marsh's pen, this country, just far enough distant to become a field for the golden dreams of many a romantic youth. Now, then, this land appeared again in a new dress, 'covered with gold,' and letters filled with gold dust had arrived together with more inviting descriptions and urgent invitations by friends. The romance had developed into reality and the attraction grew to an irresistible strength, the youth talented with romantic fancy filled the ranks of the adventurers, ready with the next chance to start for the newly acquired American province, the new El Dorado, where everybody could help himself to as much of the precious metal as he pleased, without the investment of a great capital.

For nearly forty days we had uninterrupted favorable winds, being in the "trades," and, having settled down to sailor habits, time passed without notice.

General William T. Sherman, 1846

"One man, a sailor, a deserter from the Ohio, took it into his head, one night, to rob one of the volunteers, who had set up a drinking store. He had already got two bags, containing about five thousand dollars' worth of gold; but, not satisfied with them, grasped at a third, half full of dollars in silver. The jingling of the coin awoke the owner, who, springing up, gave the alarm, and, after a hot pursuit, the thief was captured, and bound to a tree until morning. At about nine, a jury of twelve miners sat to consider the case, a volunteer named Nutman officiating for Judge Lynch. Of course, he was found guilty, and sentenced to be hanged; but, some opposition being raised to depriving him of life, and a milder punishment suggested, it was finally determined that he should receive a hundred lashes on his bare back, have his ears cut off, and his head shaved, so that he might be everywhere recognised in the mining districts."

William Redmond
Ryan, 1848-9

At the peak of the Gold Rush, hundreds of ships were moored in San Francisco harbor, often just having made the trip "around the horn." Sometimes the ships were resold to miners ready to return to the "States." As often as not, they were stripped of valuables (the sails made great tents for miners) and left to rot.

THE 1848 DISCOVERY OF GOLD: THE GOLD RUSH

James W. Marshall, the lucky discoverer of gold at Coloma, came to California from Oregon in 1845, whither he had gone overland from Missouri the year before. He came to Sutter's fort, then the headquarters of all adventurers. Here he enlisted into the ranks of the California battalion under Colonel Fremont and took part in the American conquest and returned to Sutter's fort after this battalion was discharged at Los Angeles, in early summer of 1847. On an excursion trip from the fort up on the American river he came through the Culloomah basin—now Coloma— and the location, concerning the beautiful stand of sugar-pine trees, and the pleasant water power on the South Fork of the American river, found his consent and awakened his desire to build a sawmill there. Returning to the fort he tried to persuade Captain Sutter to enter into a partnership agreement by which the latter was to furnish the means, while he (Marshall) was to superintend the erection and operation of the mill. With a full equipment of workmen and tools he started for the mill site at Coloma on the 28th of August, 1847. Here we give the names of the men who were working at the mill: Peter L. Weimer, William Scott, James

Bargee, Alexander Stephens, James Brown, William Johnson and Henry Bigler. Besides these white men there were some Indians employed also.

The mill was built over a dry channel of the river which was calculated to the tail race. Marshall, being a kind of wheelwright, had constructed the "tub-wheel" and had also furnished some of the rude parts of the machinery necessary for an ordinary up-and-down sawmill. By January, 1848, the mill was about finished, the tub-wheel set in motion, and after having arranged the head-race and dam he let on the water to test the goodness of his machinery. All worked very well until it was found that the tail-race did not carry off the water fast enough, so he was compelled to deepen and widen the tail-race. In order to economize labor he ordered his men to scratch a kind of a ditch down in the middle of the dry channel, throwing only the coarser stones out of the race, then letting on the water again, it would run with velocity through the channel, washing away all the lose dirt. This was done in the night so as not to interfere with the work of the men in the daytime, and in the morning Marshall, after closing the forebay gate, thus shutting off the water, used to walk down the tail-race to inspect the work the water had done.

Here (Cape Horn) we experienced very rough weather, buffeting about under storm stay-sails, and spending nearly a month before the wind favored our passage.

General William T. Sherman, 1846

This is the oldest known photo of Sutter's Mill, the gold discovery site in Coloma. After gold was discovered, the mill was abandoned when workers left for the gold fields. Chinese and other miners camped on the mill platform as can be seen in this photo. The man in front is not Marshall or Sutter, but an unknown character, perhaps the photographer's assistant.

Library of Congress, Lawrence & Houseworth Collection

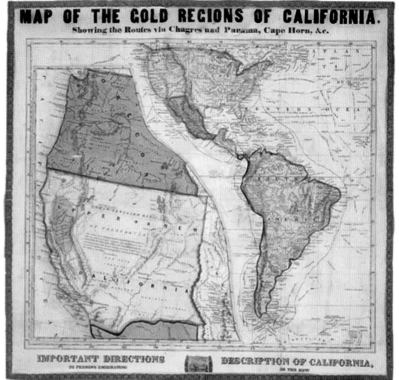

MAP OF THE GOLD REGIONS OF CALIFORNIA.
Showing the Routes via Chagres and Panama, Cape Horn, &c.

IMPORTANT DIRECTIONS   DESCRIPTION OF CALIFORNIA,

...a pebble weighing six pennyweights and eleven grains, after the best authorities, was found on the memorable day 19th of January.

"On this occasion," says the "Life and Adventures of James W. Marshall," "having strolled to the lower end of the race, he stood for a moment examining the mass of debris that had washed down, and at this juncture his eye caught the glitter of something that lay lodged in the crevice of a riffle of soft granite, some six inches under the water. His first act was to stoop and pick up the substance. It was heavy, of peculiar color, and unlike anything he had seen in the stream before."

This specimen, a pebble weighing six pennyweights and eleven grains, after the best authorities, was found on the memorable day 19th of January, in the presence of Peter L. Weimer. Marshall, after keeping it in his hand for a few minutes, reflecting and endeavoring to recall all he had heard or read concerning the various metals, but not being able to determine about its substance, handed it over to Weimer, that it was closely examined by him and Scott, and because, after some different conjectures, none of them could decide about the quality of the mineral, Weimer was ordered to take it home and have his wife boil it in saleratus water. He took the piece home with him, handed it to his wife who, as she was engaged boiling soap at the time, threw the specimen in the soap-kettle, where it remained twenty-four hours, and came out so much brighter than before.

The manner in which the mineral had stood the test convinced them of its valuable properties, whereupon Marshall, who had collected between the time two or three ounces of the precious metal, was prevailed upon to mount the mule and start for Sutter's fort to make the final test.

The following from the "Memoirs of General W. T. Sherman" will give the reader an idea that Marshall was far more excited than he would make believe:

"Captain Sutter himself related to me Marshall's account, saying that as he sat in his room at the fort one day in February or March, 1848, a knock was heard at the door, and he called out, 'come in.' In walked Marshall, who was a half crazy man at best, but then looked strangely wild. 'What is the matter, Marshall?" Marshall inquired if any one was in hearing [range], and began to peer around the room and look under the bed, when Sutter fearing that some calamity had befallen the party up at the sawmill, and that Marshall was really crazy, demanding of Marshall to explain what was the matter. At last he revealed his discovery and laid before Captain Sutter the pellicles of gold he had picked up in the ditch. At first Sutter attached little or no importance to the discovery, and told Marshall to go back to the mill, and say nothing of what he had seen, to his family or any one else.

The enormous influx of adventurous men of different nationalities to this very spot of land, the New El Dorado, undoubtedly had brought a good many daring and desperate characters, who had come for gain, in the easiest and least troublesome manner, but for gain under all eventualities.

Anable Placer Mine in the Auburn Ravine, 1853.

In those days miners would flock in crowds to catch a glimpse of that rare and blessed spectacle, a woman! Old inhabitants tell how, in a certain camp, the news went abroad early in the morning that a woman was come! They had seen a calico dress hanging out of a wagon down at the camping-ground and a shout went up when an actual, bona fide dress was discovered fluttering in the wind! The male emigrant was visible. The miners said:

"Fetch her out!"

He said: "It is my wife, gentlemen—she is sick—we have been robbed of money, provisions, everything, by the Indians—we want to rest."

"Fetch her out! We've got to see her!"

"But, gentlemen, she..."

"FETCH HER OUT!"

He "fetched her out," and they swung their hats and sent up three rousing cheers and a tiger; and they crowded around and gazed at her, and touched her dress, and listened to her voice with the look of men who listened to a memory rather than a present reality—and then they collected twenty-five hundred dollars in gold and gave it to the man, and swung their hats again and gave three more cheers, and went home satisfied.

Mark Twain, 1872

You didn't find many women in California in the 1850s, let alone at the gold mines. This 1850s photo captured a rare scene indeed.

"Yet, as it might add value to the location, he dispatched to our headquarters at Monterey—as before related—the two men with a written application for a pre-emption to the quarter section of land at Coloma."

Captain John A. Sutter's diary, kept by himself, gives on the same subject the highly interesting facts to be seen out of the following extracts:

"January 28th, 1848, Marshall arrived in the evening, it was raining very heavy, but he told me that he came on important business; after we were alone in a private room he showed me the first specimen of gold, that is he was not certain if it was gold or not, but he thought it might be; immediately I made the proof and found that it was gold. I told him even that most of all is 23 carat gold. He wished that I should come up with him immediately, but I told him that I have to give first my orders to the people in all my factories and shops.

"February 1st—Left for the saw-mill attended by a vaquero (Olympio.) Was absent 2d, 3d, 4th and 5th. I examined myself everything and picked up a few specimens of gold myself in the tailrace of the saw-mill. This gold and other which Marshall gave to me, (it was found while in my employ and wages), I told them I would a ring got made of it so soon as the goldsmith would be here. I had a talk with my employed people at the saw-mill, I told them that as they do now know that this metal is gold, I wished that they would do me the great favor and keep it secret for six weeks, because my large flour-mill at Brighton would have been in operation in such a time, which undertaking would have been a fortune to me, and unfortunately the people would not keep it a secret, and so I lost on this mill at the lowest calculation about $25,000."

While on this visit to Coloma Captain Sutter, with Marshall, assembled the Indians and bought a large tract of land about Coloma in exchange for a lot of beads and a few cotton handkerchiefs. They, under color of this Indian title, required one-third of all the gold dug on their domain, and collected at this rate until the fall of 1848, when a mining party from Oregon declined to pay "tithes," as they called it.

Mr. John Hittell, in his "Mining in the Pacific States," presents the following not enough known facts, on the great discovery:

"He made inquiries about the place where the gold was found, and subsequent inquiries about the trustworthiness of Mr. Bennett, and on the 7th of March, we find him at the mill. He had tried to induce several of his friends in San Francisco to go with him; but all thought his expedition a foolish one,

Hydraulic Mining near Auburn, 1860s.

Library of Congress, Lawrence & Houseworth Collection

On Sunday, July 23d, 1854, an old man named William Shay was most brutally murdered at Greenwood valley, El Dorado county, by one Samuel Allen. From the testimony adduced it appeared that Shay was engaged in watering his garden, when Allen came up to him, knocked him down and stamping on him until he was quite dead; after this he pounded Shay's head with stones until it was literally crushed to a jelly. After the perpetration of this fiendish murder Allen attempted to escape, but was arrested by an eyewitness of the scene, Antonio Dias. An officer started with Allen for Coloma, but had not proceeded far when he was overtaken by a large and excited crowd, who forcibly took the prisoner from his custody. An hour afterwards the dead body of the guilty man was hanging from the same oak limb, in the town of Greenwood, that had been used already on a similar occasion a few years ago, a solemn warning to malefactors. The aroused vengeance of the outraged community was not to be appeased with less than inflicting the most extreme punishment on the guilty.

Chinese and Anglo miners work side by side in the Auburn area, 1850s.

The Mormons employed by Sutter in the erection of a grist-mill at Brighton, getting the news of their brethren's result struck for higher wages to which Sutter yielded, until they asked ten dollars a day which he refused, and the two mills on which he had spent so much money were never built and fell into decay.

and he had to go alone. At the mill he found that there was some talk about gold and persons would go about looking for pieces of it, but no one was engaged in mining and the work of the mill was going on as usual.

But Marshall anxiously guarding his supposed treasure— after most all laborers had left their work—threatened to shoot everybody attempting to dig and gather the gold on his and Sutter's claim; but these men had sense enough to know, or found it out, that if placer gold was found at Coloma, it would also exist further down, and they gradually prospected further on, until they reached what is now known as Mormon Island, fifteen miles below, where they discovered the richest placers on earth. The Mormons employed by Sutter in the erection of a grist-mill at Brighton, getting the news of their brethren's result struck for higher wages to which Sutter yielded, until they asked ten dollars a day which he refused, and the two mills on which he had spent so much money were never built and fell into decay; but all the hands went to join the miners at Mormon Island, thus giving the place the name."

The first published notice of gold discovery appeared in the *Californian* on the 15th of March, nearly two months after it took place. We give it here:

"Gold Mine Found.—In the newly-made raceway of the sawmill recently erected by Captain Sutter, on the American fork, gold has been found in considerable quantities. One person brought thirty dollars' worth to New Helvetia [Sacramento], gathered there in a short time. California, no doubt, is rich in mineral wealth; great chances here for scientific capitalists. Gold has been found in almost every part of the country."

The discovery of gold at Coloma was almost a signal throughout the country, and soon it was answered by finding of gold on many other streams. The circumstances accompanying the first gold mining on the Calaveras, Mokelumne, Stanislaus, Yuba, Feather, Trinity, Klamath and Scott rivers, which with the American, form the principal streams along which mining has been carried on, are of historical interest.

Captain Charles M. Weber, of Tuleburg (Stockton), fitted out another prospecting party, of which a number were Si-yak-um-na Indians, and undertook the exploration of the mountains north of the Stanislaus river. This party, composed of inexperienced miners, likewise proceeded north from the Stanislaus river, but came nearer making a failure than a success, until the Mokelumne river was reached. By more delib-

Mining operation in the Auburn area, 1850s.

"My Dear Wife,

I find myself minus of a sufficient sum of gold in consequence of this trip to have carried me home I was more unfortunate in this than my comrades, for I lost my horse in the mountains, which cost upwards of a hundred dollars But in these losses I am not alone, for thousands here have experienced the same fate, so that you see I have an abundance of miserable consolations."

Truly Yours,
E. A. Spooner,
August 25, 1850

Chinese Camp in California. The Chinese, in the Gold Rush days of California, acted as miners, cooks, and laundry men. In the late 1860s they were also the chief laborers on the Central Pacific Railroad.

"Hearing a commotion outside, we proceeded to ascertain its cause, and discovered a tall mountaineer complaining of a loss he had just sustained. He had encamped in a field, at about a mile from Mr. Weaver's trading-store; and, being alone, had left the place for about a quarter of an hour, to look after his horses. He had about nine pounds' weight of gold tied up in a leathern bag, which he left in his tent, and which, on his return, he discovered had been stolen during his brief absence. He came to offer the half of it to anybody who should enable him to recover the bag. He was an Oregon man, and had a wife and large family depending upon the product of his labour at the mines, so that his case was a very hard one. He never got back a grain of the gold; the thief, whoever he was, getting clear away with it, and avoiding detection."

William Redmond
Ryan
1848-1849

erately searching here, the first gold was found in the region of the country afterwards known as the "Southern mines," so called to distinguish them from the mines more easily to be approached from Sacramento. Prospecting further on brought to light, that gold was to be found in every stream and gulch between the Mokelumne and American rivers; but no location was made until reaching the divide of the latter stream, where they commenced work in earnest on what is since known as Weber creek. As soon as the Indians accompanying the expedition had learned how to prospect, Captain Weber sent them back to their chief Jose Jesus, the Captain's friend, with instructions to prospect the Stanislaus and neighboring rivers for gold and report the results to Major Domo at Tuleburgh. Not a long time after the captain was informed with the exciting news that his Indians had found gold in quantities everywhere between the Calaveras and Stanislaus rivers. He immediately returned home, fitted out the Stockton Mining Company, and inaugurated the working of those afterward famous mines: Murphy's Camp, Sullivan's Diggings, Sansovina Bar, Woods Creek and Angel's Camp all derived their names from members of that pioneer company.

"Toward the close of June, 1848, the gold fever being at its height, by Colonel Mason's orders, I made preparations for his trip to the newly discovered gold mines at Sutter's Fort. I selected four good soldiers, with Aaron, Colonel Mason's black servant, and a good outfit of horses and pack animals; we started by the usually traveled route for Yerba Buena (San Francisco). There Captain Folsom and two other citizens joined our party. The first difficulty was to cross the bay to Saucelito. Folsom, as quarter-master, had a sort of scow with a large sail, and by means of her and infinite labor we managed to get the load of horses, etc., safely crossed to Saucelito. We followed in a more comfortable schooner. Having safely landed our horses and mules we packed up and rode to San Rafael mission, stopping with Don Timateo Murphy. The next day's journey took us to Bodega, where a man by the name of Stephen Smith lived, who had the only steam saw-mill in California. We spent a day very pleasantly with him, and learned that he had come to the country some years before, at the personal advice of Daniel Webster, who had informed him, that sooner or later the United States would be in possession of California, and that in consequence it would become a great country. From Bodega we traveled to Sonoma, and spent a day with General Vallejo. From Sonoma by the way of Napa, Suisun, and Vaca's ranch,

Northern California had a large Chinese population during and after the gold rush. Chinese miners also became part of the huge labor force required to build the railroads.

Courtesy of the Folsom Historical Society

"*My Dear Wife,*

I never saw such myriads of flowers as California produces, before. The face of the Earth is litterally covered with them. In fact two thirds of the whole verdure that covers the ground, are flowers. And some of the valleys thus covered, with various coloured flowers predominating here and there, afford one of the most pleasing views that you can well imagine. And O that you could just be here one short week to enjoy them with me !!!

...we find the labor of the five days amounted to $188.00 each, or something over thirty seven dollars pr day, pr man. If this success would continue, I would be with you in time to hold a hearty thanks giving next fall, at its annual occurrance. Remember me affectionately to Father and Mother, and Sisters. And believe me truly thine own."

E. A. Spooner,
April, 1849

A quartz mine near Downieville where four young men are reducing a slate bank for its gold content.

...we reached the Sacramento river opposite to Sutter's embarcadero. The only means of crossing over was by an Indian dugout canoe.

crossing the tules, we reached the Sacramento river opposite to Sutter's *embarcadero*. The only means of crossing over was by an Indian dugout canoe. After all things and persons were safely crossed, the horses were driven in the water, being guided ahead by a man in the canoe. Of course, the animals at first refused to take to the water, and it was nearly a day's work to get them across; and even then, the trouble was not over, some of the animals escaped in the woods and thick undergrowth that lined the river, but we secured enough to reach Fort Sutter, three miles back from the *embarcadero*; where we encamped at the slough or pond near the fort. On application, Captain Sutter sent some Indians back into the bushes who recovered and brought back all our animals.

"At that time there was not the sign of a habitation there or thereabouts, except the fort, and an old adobe house east of the fort, known as the "Hospital." These rooms were used by Captain Sutter himself, and by his people; he had a blacksmith's shop, a carpenter's shop, etc., and other rooms where the women made blankets. He had horses, cattle and sheep, and of those he gave liberally and without price to all in need. He caused to be driven into our camp a beef and some sheep, which were slaughtered for our use.

"July 5th, 1848, we commenced our journey toward the mines, and reached, after a hot and dusty ride, Mormon Island.

"When Colonel Mason and party reached Mormon Island, they found about three hundred Mormons there at work; most of them were discharged soldiers from the Mexican war. As soon as the fame of the discovery of gold spread, the Mormons naturally went to Mormon Island. Clark, of Clark's Point, one of the elders, was there also, and nearly all of the Mormons who had come out in the sailing vessel *Brooklyn*, which left New York in 1845, with Sam Brannan as leader. Sam Brannan was on hand as the high-priest, collecting the tithes. As soon as the news spread that the governor was there, persons came to see us, and volunteered all kinds of information, illustrating it by samples of the gold, which was of a uniform kind—scale gold, bright and beautiful. I remember that Mr. Clark was in camp talking to Colonel Mason about matters and things generally, when he inquired: 'Governor, what business has Sam Brannan

Miners began extracting gold from Spanish Flat as early as 1848. The Spanish Flat area was still producing gold well into the 1940s. Black miners worked alongside white miners in this photo. Blacks made up a very small percentage of California's population in the 1840s and 1850s. Historians estimate that in the early 1850s, there were between 200 and 300 blacks in the gold fields held as slaves. Most of these were brought to the state before November 1849, when the state's constitution was adopted and California was declared a free (non-slave) state. Many of these slaves were eventually able to purchase their freedom, or their freedom was granted by their owners. Places like Negro Hill, Negro Bar, and Negro Flat attest to the presence of blacks in California. There are over 30 locations in the state with names including "nigger" or "negro." Photo 1852.

This gold and other which Marshall gave to me, (it was found while in my employ and wages), I told them I would a ring got made of it so soon as the goldsmith would be here.

Captain Sutter, 1848

Courtesy of the California History Room, California State Library, Sacramento, CA

Crusty old miners hard at work in the early 1850s.

Marshall anxiously guarding his supposed treasure threatened to shoot everybody attempting to dig and gather the gold on his and Sutter's claim; but these men had sense enough to know, or found it out, that if placer gold was found at Coloma, it would also exist further down.

to collect the tithes here?' Clark admitted that Brannan was the head of the Mormon church in California. Colonel Mason answered: 'Brannan has a perfect right to collect the tithes, if you Mormons are fool enough to pay the tax.' 'Then,' said Clark, 'I, for one, won't pay any longer.' And Colonel Mason added: 'This is public land, and the gold is the property of the United States; all of you are trespassers, but as the government is benefitted by your getting out the gold I do not intend to interfere.' I understand afterward, that from that time the payment of the tithes ceased, but Brannan had already collected enough to hire Sutter's hospital and to open a store there, in which he made more money than any merchant in California during that summer and fall.

"The next day we continued our journey and reached Coloma, the place where gold had been first discovered, about noon. Only few miners were at work there, by reason of Marshall and Sutter's claim to the site. There stood the saw-mill unfinished, the dam and tail-race just as they were left when the Mormons ceased work. Marshall and his family of wife and half a dozen tow-headed children were there, living in a house made of clapboards.

"Here, also, were shown many specimens of gold, of a courser grain than that found at Mormon Island. We crossed the American river to its north side, and visited many small camps of men in what were called the 'dry diggings.' Some of these diggings were extremely rich; sometimes a lucky fellow would hit on a 'pocket,' and collect several thousand dollars in a few days; and then again would be shifting about from place to place 'prospecting,' and spending all he made. Little stores were being opened at every point, where flour, bacon, etc., were sold—everything being a dollar a pound, and a meal usually cost three dollars. Nobody paid for a bed, for he slept on the ground, without fear of cold or rain.

"I advised the colonel to allow Captain Folsom to purchase and send to Washington a large sample of the commercial gold in general use, and to pay for the same out of the money in his hands, known as the 'Civil fund,' arising from the duties collected at the several ports in California. He consented to this, and Captain Folsom bought an oyster can full, at ten dollars an ounce, which was the rate of value at which it was then received at the custom-house. Folsom was further instructed to contract with some vessel to carry the messenger to South America, where he could take the English steamer as far east as Jamaica, with a conditional charter, giving increased pay if the vessel would catch the October steamer. Folsom chartered the bark *La Lambayecana*, owned and navigated by Henry D. Cooke, who has since been the governor of the District of Columbia. He telegraphed to the War Department his arrival; but so many delays had occurred, that he did not reach Washington in time to have the matter embraced in the President's regular message

Gold Mine Found.—In the newly-made raceway of the sawmill recently erected by Captain Sutter, on the American fork, gold has been found in considerable quantities. One person brought thirty dollars' worth to New Helvetia, gathered there in a short time. California, no doubt, is rich in mineral wealth; great chances here for scientific capitalists. Gold has been found in almost every part of the country."

Californian March 15th, 1848

Near Nevada City in 1852 dozens of miners work their claims side by side.

Mormon Island was home to many a miner in its day, but many pioneers chose other work, like the 1850s farmer above who's seeding his field. Mormon Island was flooded after Folsom Dam was built. At low water, ruins of the original settlement can be found and explored.

...old vessels, laid up for years, and half rotten, or forgotten entirely at the moorings, were brought to life again; a new coppering and other most necessary repairing was done as fast as possible, the vessel fitted up as a passenger boat and advertised as a fast sailing vessel in best order, awaiting passengers for California.

of 1848, as we had calculated. Still, the President made it the subject of a special message, and thus became *official* what had before reached the world only in very indefinite shape. Then began that great development and the emigration to California, by land and by sea, of 1849 and 1850."

The seaport cities as well as the frontier post of the far west, early in 1849, became the rendezvous places of thousands of people, and their assemblage and the purpose for which they came, gave birth to many hitherto unknown branches of industry at these places. Here all the old horses, mules, oxen and cows, together with old wagons of every description, were brought to these fitting-out stations and found a ready market and sale; the emigrants on their journey being compelled to pay the highest prices for all things of necessity. There, old vessels, laid up for years, and half rotten, or forgotten entirely at the moorings, were brought to life again; a new coppering and other most necessary repairing was done as fast as possible, the vessel fitted up as a passenger boat and advertised as a fast sailing vessel in best order, awaiting passengers for California, and every one of them were filled with passengers who were willing to risk the old crafts, being all anxious to reach the far destination as fast as possible.

Many of the adventurers who were trying to make fortunes on this coast had an idea that this country was lacking of everything, and they brought with them all the necessities of life; all the implements, tools and machinery for starting most every trade; supplies were taken along to open stores of every description; printing presses and all the supplemental parts, to bring the blessings of the news to the new country, whole houses, in all their parts, ready to be put up; one wing of Mrs. Perry's hotel at Salmon Falls, El Dorado county, came around Cape Horn. And even the first steamboat ever run on the Sacramento river was imported that way by the excited adventurer. We give the following from a Boston newspaper, published as a "Recollection of the late Edward Everett;" the writer of the articles calls himself one of the party:

"After a six months' passage we arrived in California, moored our ship along the mud banks of Benicia and there built a steamboat with the material which we had purchased in Boston. It was a flat-bottomed boat, and a clumsy affair, but it was propelled by the aid of steam and with paddle wheels, and that specimen of our work we named *Edward Everett, Jr.* This steamer was the first one that ever navigated the Sacramento river; and it should be known in history that through the kindness of Edward Everett, the orator and statesman, the one

"We learn that an attempt was made last week to rob a Chinaman who supplies several companies on the South Fork of the American river with fresh meat, as he was returning to White Rock, by three well known river thieves. The attempt was made in open day on a much frequented trail. The Chinaman made his escape by sliding down a precipitous mountain about fifty feet deep without other injuries than tearing his clothes into ribbons. These outrages are becoming quite common, and it is time that some stringent measures should be taken to have the scoundrels arrested."

Mountain Democrat,
of September 22d, 1855

Courtesy of the Folsom Historical Society

Chinese laborers were numerous. Even in the harshest conditions, they enjoyed their tea and stayed healthier than other pioneers. Because the tea water was boiled, the Chinese often escaped the ravages of Cholera and other water-born diseases.

Monongahia, a sloop of war, built in 1863, was Admiral Farraguts Flagship, Battle of Mobile Bay. It was destroyed by fire, 1908.

Steve Crandell Collection. Restoration by Steve Crandell

One day we sailed parallel with a French sloop-of-war, and it was sublime to watch the two ships rising and falling in those long deep swells of the ocean.

General William T. Sherman, 1846

hundred and fifty adventurers were proud to place his name on the sides of their rude craft, a wonder in those days, when only sailing vessels ascended the river."

Thus the early gold-hunters started out on their voyage provided with everything the boldest imagination could think of; equipped, not as the law directed quite, but as the inclination dictated them. The trip around Cape Horn was tiresome and absorbed much time; but, after all, the travelers that took their choice of this route found that they had done the best, and in most every line of comparison the advantage was on their side. The overland travelers starting with insufficient knowledge of their own necessities as well as the character of the country they had to traverse, had their wagons loaded down to the utmost with not much less of all kinds of stuff than the former class, soon enough found themselves concerned with difficulties, and experience was the master that taught them the right way. Most of the emigrants were overloaded with provisions to such an extent that it soon became a burden to them and their pulling animals; but short, they resolved to throw the burden overboard, and as others followed the same example, there could be found along the different emigrant roads piled up like cordwood, all different articles of food, particularly hams, bacon and flour-barrels, and on more difficult points of the roads there were wagons loaded with goods left behind, on account of an insufficiency of pulling animals, those from the abandoned wagons being required more necessary for the balance of the rigging.

The number of emigrants from the Western States that set out in the spring of 1849, can only be approximately estimated, varying between 50,000 and 80,000. Most of the emigrants, coming by the Santa Fe route, went to the southern mines; those entering the territory by the Pitt river route went to the northern part; the Truckee river pass led down to the mines on Bear, Yuba and neighboring rivers; and the Carson pass brought those hunting the El Dorado down to the American river, and being satisfied here, they called it *El Dorado*.

A third route to reach the El Dorado on the Pacific coast was by the way of the Isthmus of Panama, and the emigrants who had selected the same, without any doubt calculating on the shortest and cheapest way, found they had made a miscalculation, and were in the worst condition of all the emigrants; for after being landed at Chargres, Navy Bay, or some other harbor, together with their baggage and eventually other outfit, they had to go across the Isthmus either afoot or on mule's back and await the arrival of the next steamer. Thus from 5,000 to 8,000 American emigrants were compelled to take involuntary

The first occasion where this historical oak tree had been selected to serve for the same purpose, happened in 1851; James Graham, from Baltimore, treacherously had invited an old denizen of Greenwood valley, by the name of Lesly, a well respected gentleman, to go with him on a prospecting trip, where he filled his head with buckshot, and thinking his victim dead, he fled. Lesly, however, did not die on the spot; though fatally wounded, he crawled to the next cabin, being that of Tom Burch, in Coloma canyon, whom he informed of what had happened; the people thus alarmed, turned out in pursuit of the assassin, caught him at Uniontown, and brought him back to Greenwood valley, where a jury of twelve men was sworn in before whom he was tried, found guilty and immediately taken to the mentioned oak tree, standing on the lot now owned by Mr. Ricci, where he was hung without ceremonies.

The "A.R. Tucker" a bark/whaler, was built in 1851.

Steve Crandell Collection, Restoration by Steve Crandell

Steve Crandell Collection. Restoration by Steve Crandell

The "California," a Barkentine, was built in 1842, in New Bedford, Massachusetts. It was one of hundreds of sailing vessels from "the States" that sailed round the Horn to bring adventurers to the new El Dorado.

The people endeavoring to put a stop to those crimes were often enough compelled to take the law in their own hands, as may be seen out of the case which originated the sobriquet of Hangtown for the village of Placerville.

lodgings up to the time when their chances would turn up to move further on, and not being accustomed to the tropical climate, malarial fever, cholera, etc., were ravaging badly in their ranks. But the few steamers could not give passage to one-fourth of the people arriving every week, the price for tickets run up immensely. Vessels of every description came flocking into Panama harbor to get their share of this travel; unloading their cargo if necessary and making some arrangements for the transportation of passengers — all ready to be either chartered or sold to a company of emigrants.

The number of arrivals on the water-way at San Francisco, from April 12th, 1849, to February 28th, 1859, was 43,824. The emigrant road from the Carson Pass down into El Dorado alone, saw passing over it, if not more, as least as many arriving emigrants as those who landed at San Francisco.

The estimated production of gold in the United States from 1848 to 1873 is $1,240,750,000, of which California contributed $1,083,075,000.

By the early 1850s there were stations with food and accommodations along the most traveled Sierra Nevada routes. Prior to that, emigrants had to survive on their wits and determination. Photo, Slippery Ford House, 1860s.

Chapter 3: The Donner Party - a Tale of Survival

[The words of survivor Eliza P. Donner Houghton] In camp that night, Mr. Stanton outlined our course to the settlement, and consented to lead the train across the Sierra Nevada Mountains. Frost in the air and snow on the distant peaks warned us against delays; yet, notwithstanding the need of haste, we were obliged to rest our jaded teams. Three yoke of oxen had died from exhaustion within a week, and several of those remaining were not in condition to ascend the heavy grades before them.

Frost in the air and snow on the distant peaks warned us against delays...

Heavy snows can plague travelers over the Sierras throughout the year. This snowy scene on the summit of the Sierra Nevada Mountains was taken on June 15, in the 1860s.

With sickening anguish the first morsels were prepared... Not one touched flesh of kindred body... Death would have been preferable to that awful meal, had relentless fate not said: "Take, eat that ye may live. Eat, lest ye go mad and leave your work undone!"

Up and up we toiled until we reached an altitude of six thousand feet, and were within about ten miles of our companions at the lake, when the intense cold drove us into camp on Prosser.

The following morning the ground was covered with snow two or three feet in depth, which had to be shovelled from the exposed beds before their occupants could rise.

Father's face [George Donner] was very grave. His morning caress had all its wonted tenderness, but the merry twinkle was gone from his eye, and the gladsome note from his voice. For eight consecutive days, the fatal snow fell with but few short intermissions.

Some of the poor creatures had perished under bushes where they sought shelter. A few had become bewildered and strayed; others were found under trees in snow pits, which they themselves had made by walking round and round the trunks to keep from being snowed under. These starvelings were shot to end their sufferings, and also with the hope that their hides and fleshless bones might save the lives of our snow-beleaguered party. Every part of the animals was saved for food. The locations of the carcasses were marked so that they could be brought piece by piece into camp; and even the green hides were spread against the huts to serve in case of need.

Uncle Jacob, the first to die, was older than my father, and had been in miserable health for years. Like a tired child falling asleep, was James Smith's death.

Our camp having been thus depleted by death, Noah James helped John Baptiste to dig for the carcasses of the cattle. It was weary work, for the snow was higher than the level of the guide marks, and at times they searched day after day and found no trace of hoof or horn. The little field mice that had crept into camp were caught then and used to ease the pangs of hunger. Also pieces of beef hide were cut into strips, singed, scraped, boiled to the consistency of glue, and swallowed with an effort; for no degree of hunger could make the saltless, sticky substance palatable. Marrowless bones which had already been boiled and scraped, were now burned and eaten, even the bark and twigs of pine were chewed in the vain effort to soothe the gnawings which made one cry for bread and meat.

Snowy Christmas brought us no "glad tidings," and New Year's Day no happiness.

The natives were often found traveling on snow shoes. It didn't take long for the early settlers to also began to use both snowshoes and skis to get around. In this early 1860s photos, trappers set a bear trap, one of many ways in which the grizzly bear was driven from the Sierra Nevada Mountains.

"The bones of those who had died and been devoured by the miserable ones that still survived, were lying around their tents and cabins. Bodies of men, women and children, with half the flesh torn from them, lay on every side. A woman sat by the side of the body of her husband, who had just died, cutting out his tongue; the heart she had already taken out, broiled and eat !

California Star of the 10th April, 1847

Travel was frequently treacherous. These teamsters approaching Pyramid Peak in the 1860s were lucky to find only light snow.

"So changed had the immigrants become, that when the party sent out arrived with food, some of them cast it aside, and seemed to prefer the putrid human flesh that still remained. The day before the party arrived, one of the immigrants took a child of about four years of age in bed with him, and devoured the whole before morning, and the next day he eat another about the same age before noon.

California Star of the 10th April, 1847

Then like a smile from God, came another sunny day which not only warmed and dried us thoroughly but furnished a supply of water from dripping snowbanks.

The twenty-first was also bright, and John Baptiste went on snowshoes with messages to the lake camp. He found its inmates in a more pitiable condition than we were.

Days passed. No food in camp except an unsavory beef hide—pinching hunger called for more. Again John Baptiste and Noah James went forth in anxious search for marks of our buried cattle. They made excavations, then forced their hand-poles deep, deeper into the snow, but in vain their efforts—the nail and hook at the points brought up no sign of blood, hair, or hide. In dread unspeakable they returned, and said:

"We shall go mad; we shall die! It is useless to hunt for the cattle; but the *dead, if they could be reached, their bodies might keep us alive.*"

"No," replied father and mother, speaking for themselves. "No, part of a hide still remains. When it is gone we will perish, if that be the alternative."

It will be remembered that the Forlorn Hope was the party of fifteen which, as John Baptiste reported to us, made the last unaided attempt to cross the mountains.

Words cannot picture, nor mind conceive, more torturing hardships and privations than were endured by that little band on its way to the settlement. It left the camp on the sixteenth of December, with scant rations for six days, hoping in that time to force its way to Bear Valley and there find game. But the storms which had been so pitiless at the mountain camps followed the unprotected refugees with seemingly fiendish fury. After the first day from camp, its members could no longer keep together on their marches. The stronger broke the trail, and the rest followed to nightcamp as best they could.

Mr. Graves, who was also breathing heavily, when told by Mr. Eddy that he was dying, replied that he did not care. He, however, called his daughters, Mrs. Fosdick and Mary Graves,

On the seventeenth, the chief with much difficulty procured, for Mr. Eddy, a gill of pine nuts which the latter found so nutritious that the following morning, on resuming travel, he was able to walk without support.

In 1856, a Mr. Swift and Mr. Watson began operating the Strawberry Valley House as a hostelry. In 1859, a Mr. Berry managed station operations at Strawberry and established a partnership with Mr. Swan to build a road over the mountain. Berry also served as the station keeper when the Pony Express began. One source suggests the station's name, Strawberry, came from Berry's alleged practice of feeding travelers' horses with straw, when the owners had paid for hay.

The Lake House at Lake Tahoe, 1860s.

It is useless to hunt for the cattle; but the dead, if they could be reached, their bodies might keep us alive."

to him, and by his parting injunctions, showed that he was still able to realize keenly the dangers that beset them. Remembering how their faces had paled at the suggestion of using human flesh for food, he admonished them to put aside the natural repugnance which stood between them and the possibility of life. He commanded them to banish sentiment and instinctive loathing, and think only of their starving mother, brothers, and sisters whom they had left in camp, and avail themselves of every means in their power to rescue them. He begged that his body be used to sustain the famishing, and bidding each farewell, his spirit left its bruised and worn tenement before half the troubles of the night were passed.

The crucial hour had come. Food lay before the starving, yet every eye turned from it and every hand dropped irresolute.

Mr. Eddy now fed his waning strength on shreds of his concealed bear meat, hoping that he might survive to save the giver. The rest in camp could scarcely walk and their sensations of hunger were diminishing. This condition forebode delirium and death, unless stayed by the only means at hand. It was in very truth a pitiful alternative offered to the sufferers.

With sickening anguish the first morsels were prepared and given to Lemuel Murphy, but for him they were too late.

Not one touched flesh of kindred body. Nor was there need of restraining hand, or warning voice to gauge the small quantity which safety prescribed to break the fast of the starving. Death would have been preferable to that awful meal, had relentless fate not said: "Take, eat that ye may live. Eat, lest ye go mad and leave your work undone!"

All but the Indians obeyed the mandate, and were strengthened and reconciled to prepare the remaining flesh to sustain them a few days longer on their journey.

January 1, 1847, was, to the little band of eight, a day of less distressing trials; its members resumed travel early, braced by unswerving will-power. They stopped at midday and revived strength by eating the toasted strings of their snowshoes. Mr.

Friday's Station, also known as Lakeside (Nevada), was a Pony Express stop. Friday's Station began operation in early 1860 as a franchise station on the Kingsbury Grade, a new road through the Sierra Nevada Mountains, near the Nevada-California border. Martin K. "Friday" Burke and James Washington Small managed operations at this home station for the Pony Express and later stage lines. Structures at Friday's included a one-room log cabin, a two-and-one-half-story hostelry, dining room, kitchen, storeroom, woodshed, and a roomy building that doubled as a stable and hay barn. Burke and Small conducted a profitable business at the station for several years after the demise of the Pony Express. In 1888 John Wales Averill purchased the station and surrounding property and renamed the site "Edgewood."

Warned by the sky, cautious mountaineers, together with the wild sheep, deer, and most of the birds and bears, make haste to the lowlands or foot-hills; and burrowing marmots, mountain beavers, wood rats, and such people go into winter quarters, some of them not again to see the light of day until the general awakening and resurrection of the spring in June or July. The first heavy fall is usually from about two to four feet in depth. Then, with intervals of splendid sunshine, storm succeeds storm, heaping snow on snow, until thirty to fifty feet has fallen.

John Muir, 1894

Library of Congress, Lawrence & Houseworth Collection

An 1860s cabin at Lake Angela near Donner Peak.

The old chief sent an Indian with him as a guide and support. And so that long, desperate struggle for life, and for the sake of loved ones, ended an hour before sunset, when Mr. Eddy, leaning heavily upon the Indians, halted before the door of Colonel M. D. Richey's home, thirty-five miles from Sutter's Fort.

Eddy also ate his worn out moccasins, and all felt a renewal of hope upon seeing before them an easier grade which led to night-camp where the snow was only six feet in depth.

Jay Fosdick was sinking rapidly, and Mr. Eddy resolved to take the gun and steal away from camp at dawn in search of game. Not a moving creature nor a creeping thing had crossed the trail on their journey thither; but the open country before them, and minor marks well known to hunters, had caught Mr. Eddy's eye and strengthened his determination. Mary Graves declared that she would keep up with him, and without heeding further opposition the two set out. A short distance from camp they stopped at a place where a deer had recently lain.

They had not proceeded far before they saw a large buck about eighty yards distant. Mr. Eddy raised his rifle and for some time tried to bring it to bear upon the deer, but such was his extreme weakness that he could not.

He brought the gun to his face the third time, and elevated the muzzle above the deer, let it descend until he saw the animal through the sight, when the rifle cracked.

The deer ran a short distance, then fell, and the two eager watchers hastened to it as fast as their weakened condition would allow. Mr. Eddy cut the throat of the expiring beast with his pocket-knife, and he and his companion knelt down and drank the warm blood that flowed from the wound.

The venison had been consumed. Hope had almost died in the heart of the bravest, when at the close of day on the tenth of January, twenty-five days from the date of leaving Donner Lake, they saw an Indian village at the edge of a thicket they were approaching. As the sufferers staggered forward, the Indians were overwhelmed at sight of their misery. The warriors gazed in stolid silence. The squaws wrung their hands and wept aloud. The first sense of horror having passed, those dusky mothers fed the unfortunates.

The following morning the chief sent his runners to other rancherias, en route to the settlement, telling his people of the distress of the pale-faces who were coming toward them, and who would need food. When the Forlorn Hope was ready to move on, the chief led the way, and an Indian walked on either side of each sufferer supporting and helping the unsteady feet. At each rancheria the party was put in charge of a new leader and fresh supporters.

The old chief sent an Indian with him as a guide and support. And so that long, desperate struggle for life, and for the sake of loved ones, ended an hour before sunset, when Mr. Eddy, leaning heavily upon the Indians, halted before the door of Colonel M. D. Richey's home, thirty-five miles from Sutter's Fort.

The Schooner Monterey, built by M. Turner, Benicia, California 1887. Photo 1890 at San Francisco

Chapter 4: San Francisco

MARCH 20th. [1847]—The local newspaper, the *"California Star,"* is pleased, at last, to acquiesce, very unwillingly, in the change of name from Yerba Buena to San Francisco.

MAY 28th. [1847] First grand illumination in San Francisco. This was in honor of General Taylor's great victory over the Mexicans at Buena Vista. Every building in the town, of frame or adobe, and shanty itself, shone with as much lustre as an unlimited allowance of oil and tallow could bestow. Fire-arms cracked, and bonfires blazed on all sides.

NOVEMBER 15th. [1847] "The Steamboat,"—being the only one it had no distinct name,—performed an experi-

This day a turkey flew overboard. The Captain ordered a boat to be lowered with four sailors and it was caught, but its feathers were so saturated with salt water it was deemed expedient to kill it and we had it for dinner. We have had poultry daily ever since we left New York. We have now about twelve dozen fowls and seven or eight turkeys. The Captain considers the turkeys worth thirty shillings each.

Lucy Kendall Herrick, 1852
Friday June 11th.

Fort Point was built by the U.S. Army Corps of Engineers between 1853 and 1861 to prevent entrance of a hostile fleet into San Francisco Bay. It was designed to mount 126 massive cannon. Rushed to completion at the beginning of the Civil War, Fort Point was first garrisoned in February of 1861. The fort was occupied throughout the Civil War, but more powerful rifled cannon made Fort Point obsolete. In 1886 the troops were withdrawn. The last cannon were removed about 1900. The Golden Gate Bridge was built over the top of the Fort in the 1930s. Photo 1866.

Gold was the irresistible magnet that drew human souls to the place where it lay, rudely snapping asunder the feebler ties of affection and duty.

mental trip round "Wood Island." This was but a small concern which had been brought by Mr. Leidesdorff from Sitka. It was the first vessel of the kind in San Francisco Bay, and was quite a pet or plaything in its way. Two days afterwards "the steamboat" sailed for Santa Clara. In February following it was lost in a Norther.

JANUARY 11th [1848]—Stringent resolutions were passed by the council regarding gambling. This vice had been growing in popular favor. Besides heavily fining parties engaged in gambling, one of the resolutions authorized the authorities "to seize for the benefit of the town all the money found on a gambling table where cards are played." If this had been in force a short time afterwards, when the gold discoveries had enriched thousands, and the reckless miners hurried to San Francisco to spend their gains in the great public gaming saloons of the period, the town in a single night would have become wealthy.

But at the next meeting of the council these resolutions were all repealed.

MARCH 15th.—About this period the population of the town was ascertained by the Board of School Trustees, in canvassing the place for educational purposes, to be, 575 male and 177 female adults, and 60 children of ages to attend school, making a total of 812. Adding the number of infants and children still too young to attend school, the whole number of inhabitants amounted to about 850. The buildings of all kinds numbered 200. There were two large hotels in the place, besides boarding and public houses, and houses attached to ten-pin alleys, billiard saloons; so that the town was becoming one of some consequence, and was assuming the pretensions and attractions of older, wealthier and more populous communities. Two wharves were in the course of construction, and extensive stores and warehouses had been erected.

MAY 18th.—Mr. Wm. A. Leidesdorff died of the brain fever. This gentleman was the United States vice-consul at San Francisco, and was closely connected with all the interests of the place. Minute guns were fired as the burial train moved on towards the Mission Dolores, in the churchyard of which place the body was interred.

Telegraph Hill from Vallejo Street Wharf, 1860s

On the evening of the 10th of June, 1851, a person of the name of John Jenkins feloniously entered a store on Long Wharf, and stole a safe. An alarm being raised, he was pursued. He then got into a boat, and sculled out into the bay, followed by a dozen other boats in keen pursuit. The prisoner was next taken to the rooms of the Vigilance Committee, in Battery street. At about ten o'clock of the same night, a signal was given on the bell of the Monumental Engine Company; and shortly afterwards about eight members of the committee hurried to the appointed place, and on giving the secret password were admitted. For two long hours, the committee were closely occupied in examining evidence; and soon they had no reason to doubt the prisoner's guilt. At midnight, the bell of the California Engine House was tolled, as sentence of death by hanging was passed upon the wretched man. Before the prisoner had reached the building, a score of persons seized the loose end of the rope and ran backwards, dragged the wretch along the ground and raising him to the beam. Thus they held him till he was dead. Nor did they let the body go until some hours afterwards, new volunteers relieving those who were tired of holding the rope.

The San Francisco I found upon my arrival had already been partially rebuilt and was ripe for a new conflagration. Doctor Briot has placed at my disposal the shack he put together out of odds and ends of lumber some six months ago.

This was where I made my headquarters. And here hundreds of white rats & millions of fleas in the sands near my shack kept me company in my tiny box-like residence just nine meters square. Outside, the shack was made of rough boards; within it was arranged like a ship's cabin with three bunks. A box served for a seat, a plank for a table, and a hole covered with glass for a window. On the floor was a layer of fine sand—the camping-ground of a colony of fleas which hopped around looking for a chance to make a good meal off me.

I supplied them with sustenance all evening, though I slaughtered enough of the creatures to fill a large graveyard. And by the time I was ready to retire my legs were literally covered with these blood-thirsty insects. So throwing myself down on the highest bunk I took a small bottle of alcohol and, letting my legs dangle over the sides, I rubbed them together rapidly, put on alcohol, and so got rid of all these inconvenient parasites. This was the price of sleep.

Ernest de Massey, 1850

Steamship Sacramento in San Francisco, 1860s

Early in the spring of this year, occasional intelligence had been received of the finding of gold in large quantities among the foot hills of the Sierra Nevada. Small parcels of the precious metal had also been forwarded to San Francisco, while visitors from the mines, and some actual diggers arrived, to tell the wonders of the region and the golden gains of those engaged in exploring and working it. In consequence of such representations, the inhabitants began gradually, in bands and singly, to desert their previous occupations, and betake themselves to the American River and other auriferous parts of the great Sacramento valley. Labor, from the deficiency of hands, rose rapidly in value, and soon all business and work, except the most urgent, was forced to be stopped. Seamen deserted from their ships in the bay and soldiers from the barracks. Over all the country the excitement was the same. Neither threats, punishment nor money could keep men to their most solemn engagements.

In the month of May it was computed that, at least one hundred and fifty people had left San Francisco, and every day since was adding to their number.

1848-1849. While San Francisco, like so many other parts of the country, was forsaken in the manner described in the foregoing, the neighborhood of the American River was overflowing with people, all busily engaged in gold hunting. The miners by the middle of May were estimated to be about two thousand. In another month they had increased probably to three; and, two months later, their number was supposed to be about six thousand. The vast majority of all the laboring classes in the country had certainly deserted their former pursuits, and had become miners, while a great many others-merchants and their clerks, shopkeepers and their assistants, lawyers, surgeons, officials in every department of the State, of the districts and in the towns, runaway seamen and soldiers, and a great variety of nondescript adventurers-likewise began the search for gold. The miners were by no means exclusively American. They consisted of every kindred and clan. There were already tame Indians, Mexicans from Sonora, Kanakas from the Sandwich Islands, settlers from Oregon, mixed with the usual dash of Spanish, British, German and French adventurers that had for a long time existed in California. Later months were to bring other Mexicans, Chinese, Peruvians, and Chilians, and all these before the great impending immigration of Americans and Europeans.

The story has a shady as well as a bright side, and would be incomplete unless both were shown. There happened to be

There were no kind eyes to gaze mournfully on him, hearts to feel, lips to speak softly, and hands to minister to his wants. His gains were swept away to buy a hasty and careless medical attendance; and too generally he died "unwept, unkneeled, unknown."

Gas Works and Long Bridge at Rincon Point, 1860s

Library of Congress, Lawrence & Houseworth Collection

The first Cliff House, above, was a modest structure built in 1863 by Masters Butler and Buckley. The guest register bore the names of three U.S. Presidents as well as prominent San Francisco families such as the Hearsts, Stanfords and Crockers who would drive their carriages out to Ocean Beach for horse racing and recreation. In 1881, the Cliff House was sold to Adolph Sutro, a self made millionaire, philanthropist and later a mayor of San Francisco. Seven years later, Sutro built a railroad to bring the general public to this seaside attraction. On Christmas Day 1894, the Cliff House was destroyed by fire.

On the 85th day out we have in sight an object that greatly attracted our attention & ere long the green hills of San Francisco bay began to show their highest points, & soon we were gliding smoothly along between them, down the bay, & when the order came to let go anchor, we brought up directly in front of the City amidst a fleet of vessels, of all kinds & sizes.

The buildings were mostly of cloth, some small frames were covered with it, others covered with shingles & boards, & some few good buildings were up & many more in the course of erection. The hills in all directions were covered with tents & the streets crowded with people from all parts of the world anxious to make their fortunes in a few days in this golden land of promise.

S. SHUFELT, 1850
Written from
Placerville

a "sickly season" in the autumn at the mines; and many of the miners sank under fever and diseases of the bowels. A severe kind of labor, to which most had been unaccustomed, a complete change of diet and habits, insufficient shelter, continued mental excitement, and the excesses in personal amusement and dissipation which golden gains induced, added to the natural unhealthiness that might have existed in the district. No gains could compensate a dying man for the fatal sickness engendered by his own avaricious exertions. In the wild race for riches, the invalid was neglected by old comrades still in rude health and the riotous enjoyment of all the pleasures that gold and the hope could bestow. When that was the case with old companions it could not be expected that strangers should care whether the sick man lived or died. Who forsooth among the busy throng would trouble himself with the feeble miner that had miscalculated his energies, and lay dying on the earthen floor of his tent or under the protecting branch of a tree?

About the end of May we left San Francisco almost a desert place, and such it continued during the whole summer and autumn months. Many ships with valuable cargoes had meanwhile arrived in the bay, but the seamen deserted. The goods at great expense had been somehow got landed, but there was nobody to take care of them, or remove them from the wharves where they lay exposed to the weather, and blocking up the way. The merchants who remained were in a feverish bustle. They were selling goods actually arrived at high prices, and could get no hands to assist them in removing and delivering the articles. By and bye, some of the miners came back to their old homes; but most of them were emaciated, feeble and dispirited. Here, therefore, as at the mines, the prices of labor and all necessaries rose exceedingly. The common laborer, who had formerly been content with his dollar a day, now proudly refused ten; the mechanic, who had recently been glad to receive two dollars, now rejected twenty for his day's services. It was certainly a great country, this-there was no mistake about it; and every subject was as lofty, independent, and seemingly as rich as a king.

The population of a great State was suddenly flocking in upon them, and no preparations had hitherto been made for its

Within the first eight weeks after the "diggings" had been fairly known, two hundred and fifty thousand dollars had reached San Francisco in gold dust, and within the next eight weeks, six hundred thousand more.

Train wreck near the Cliff House, late 1860s.

This 1860s San Francisco scene shows "What Cheer House," a hotel opened in 1852 by R. B. Woodward and destroyed by the fire of 1906. It catered to men only, permitted no liquor, and housed San Francisco's first free library and first museum. Next to it the "Original House," advertises "Baths 25Cts," and "Wines & Liquors Wholesale & Retail."

All classes gambled in those days, from the starched white neck-clothed professor of religion to the veriest black rascal that earned a dollar for blackening massa's boots.

reception. Building lots had to be surveyed, and streets graded and planked —hills levelled-hollows, lagoons, and the bay itself piled, capped, filled up and planked-lumber, bricks, and all other building materials, provided at most extraordinarily high prices-houses built, finished and furnished-great warehouses and stores erected wharves run far out into the sea-number-less tons of goods removed from shipboard, and delivered and shipped anew every where-and ten thousand other things had all to be done without a moment's unnecessary delay. Long before these things were completed, the sand-hills and barren ground around the town were overspread with a multitude of canvas, blanket and bough-covered tents,—the bay was alive with shipping and small craft carrying passengers and goods backwards and forwards,—the unplanked, ungraded, unformed streets, (at one time moving heaps of dry sand and dust; at another, miry abysses, whose treacherous depths sucked in horse and dray, and occasionally man himself,) were crowded with human beings from every corner of the universe. And every body made money, and was suddenly growing rich.

Gambling saloons, glittering like fairy palaces, like them suddenly sprang into existence, studding nearly all sides of the plaza, and every street in its neighborhood. As if intoxicating drinks from the well plenished and splendid bar they each contained were insufficient to gild the scene, music added its loudest, if not its sweetest charms; and all was mad, feverish mirth, where fortunes were lost and won, upon the green cloth, in the twinkling of an eye.

FEBRUARY 28th. The steamship *"California,"* being the first of the line of mail steamers along the coast, arrived. The citizens hailed her appearance with many cheers and other demonstrations of joy. General Persifer F. Smith, a passenger on this vessel, came to take command of the Pacific division of the military department of the United States, which comprehends Oregon and California.

JULY – Nearly two hundred square rigged vessels lay at anchor about the end of July. Hosts of passengers by these vessels, after staying but a little while in the town, hurried off to the diggings. Meanwhile, others who had been fortunate were returning from the mines with bags of gold dust, to squander in gambling, in drinking and all manner of thoutless extravagance and dissipation. Gambling, which previously had been carried

A short experience of the mines had satisfied most of the citizens of San Francisco that, in vulgar parlance, all was not gold that glittered, and that hard work was not easy, — sorry truisms for weak or lazy men.

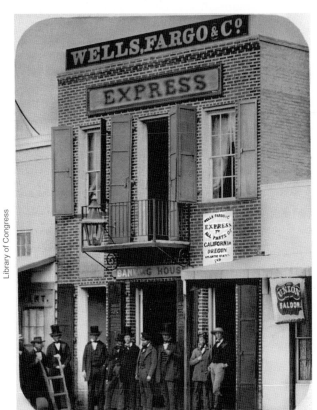

Wells Fargo & Company Express Office and the Union Saloon, San Francisco, 1860s.

JULY 15th [1848]
The affair of the
"hounds" came to
an end. This was an
association of young men.
It was virtually a gang of
public robbers. The members
assumed a kind of military
discipline, and occasionally paraded
the streets with flags displayed and
drum and fife playing. They attacked
the tents of inoffensive people, chiefly
foreigners, and if they could not extort
money from the owners or inmates
by threats, tore them down to the
ground, and stole or destroyed money,
jewels, and every thing valuable
on the premises. These outrages,
perpetrated usually at night, when
the more peaceable citizens had
retired to rest, were so frequent that
the "hounds" became a terror to all
well-disposed people of the town.
They invaded the stores, taverns,
and houses of Americans themselves;
and rudely demanded whatever they
desired. They could not be refused,
for their numbers were so great, that
nobody durst resist them. The town
was paralyzed with terror, and the
"hounds," committed the most violent
and cruel outrages in open defiance
of the law and common humanity.
Nine were [caught and] convicted
and sentenced to various periods of
imprisonment and considerable fines,
and the town was purged for a while
of the more violent ruffians that had
infested it.

The rapid growth of San Francisco and other Northern California cities required a huge amount of lumber. Nearby redwood forests were harvested with gusto to satisfy the area's voracious appetite.

California State Archives

on to so great an extent, was now beginning to be developed on a still larger scale. Saloons, at the public tables of which every variety of game was to be found, arose in all quarters of the town, where play was carried on during the whole twenty-four hours, and where the gross amount of money or gold dust staked was enormous. It might almost be said that the same spirit of gambling or speculation reigned in every department of business; and prices rose and fell, and fortunes were made, and lost, and made again, according to the "play" of the parties engaged.

The gamblers at the public saloons staked such bags, or were supplied with money upon them by the "banks," till the whole was exhausted. There were few regular houses erected, for neither building materials nor sufficient labor were to be had; but canvas tents, or houses of frame, served the immediate needs of the place. Seamen deserted their vessels, as a matter of course, so soon as they dropped anchor in the bay, and hastened to the mines. Society, not merely there, but in San Francisco, was in a state of utter disorganization, which became worse and more terrible as the autumn and winter months brought new thousands of immigrants upon the place. Thefts, robberies, murders, and other outrages of the most desperate and criminal nature were taking place, and there were no proper officials to take cognizance of them, and bring the offenders to justice.

By the beginning of 1849, the population of San Francisco had increased to two thousand. Two months later it was probably about three thousand; whilst in July, when the riots and outrages of the "hounds" came to a height, it might be nearly five thousand.

1849. The population of the State, and of San Francisco in particular, had been largely increasing during the last six months. Between the 1st of January, 1849, and the 30th of June following, it was estimated that fifteen thousand had been added to the population of the country; of which number nearly ten thousand came by sea, and landed at San Francisco. Only about two hundred of these were females. The next half year gave an average of four thousand immigrants per month, by sea alone, about five hundred of whom, in all, were females; and the whole of which numbers landed at San Francisco. An immense number of Americans came direct from the Atlantic States, around Cape Horn, or by way of Panama, while many foreigners also arrived from China and from various parts of Europe. Hitherto the departures were comparatively few.

Assembling the deck of the Monitor Comanche. The USS Comanche, a 1335-ton Passaic class monitor, was assembled in San Francisco, California from parts prefabricated at Jersey City, New Jersey. In 1863, the prefabricated parts were shipped on the sailing ship Aquila. The Aquila was sunk in San Francisco. The parts were salvaged and the Comanche was commissioned in 1865 soon after the Civil War. She was one of only two ironclads stationed on the West Coast for nearly twenty five years.

Library of Congress, Lawrence & Houseworth Collection

Once I dined in San Francisco with the family of a pioneer, and talked with his daughter, a young lady whose first experience in San Francisco was an adventure, though she herself did not remember it, as she was only two or three years old at the time. Her father said that, after landing from the ship, they were walking up the street, a servant leading the party with the little girl in her arms. And presently a huge miner, bearded, belted, spurred, and bristling with deadly weapons —just down from a long campaign in the mountains, evidently-barred the way, stopped the servant, and stood gazing, with a face all alive with gratification and astonishment. Then he said, reverently:

"Well, if it ain't a child!" And then he snatched a little leather sack out of his pocket and said to the servant: "There's a hundred and fifty dollars in dust, there, and I'll give it to you to let me kiss the child!"

Mark Twain, 1872

In the 1850s, hundreds of ships were simply abandoned to rot in San Francisco harbor while the sailors raced to the diggings in search of their fortunes.

"SERIOUS DIFFICULTY. —A difficulty occurred on the race-course yesterday evening, in which a man named Edward Graves was supposed to be wounded. One Kirk was betting at Monte, when a dispute arose, pistols were drawn, and Graves shot in the abdomen. Kirk has been arrested."

Sir Henry Vere Huntley, 1856

Altogether nearly forty thousand immigrants landed at San Francisco during 1849. It will be remembered also that somewhere about thirty thousand American immigrants had reached California across the plains, many of whom ultimately settled in San Francisco. Therefore, it may be reasonably estimated, that, at the close of 1849, the population of the town numbered, at least, twenty, and probably nearer twenty-five thousand souls. A very small proportion of these were females a still smaller one, children of either sex; while the vast majority of inhabitants were adult males, in the early prime of manhood. This circumstance naturally tended to give a peculiar character to the aspect of the place and habits of the people.

In the miserable apologies for houses, surrounded by heaps and patches of filth, mud and stagnant water, the strange mixed population carried on business, after a fashion. The great recognized orders of society were tumbled topsy-turvy. Doctors and dentists became draymen, or barbers, or shoe-blacks; lawyers, brokers and clerks, turned waiters, or auctioneers, or perhaps butchers; merchants tried laboring and lumping, while laborers and lumpers changed to merchants. The idlest might be tempted, and the weakest were able, to do something—to drive a nail in frame buildings; lead a burdened mule, keep a stall, ring a bell, or run a message. Adventurers, merchants, lawyers, clerks, tradesmen, mechanics, and every class in turn kept lodging-houses, eating and drinking houses, billiard rooms and gambling saloons, or single tables at these; they dabbled in "beach and water lots," fifty-vara blocks, and new town allotments over the whole country; speculated in flour, beef; pork and potatoes; in lumber and other building materials; in dry goods and soft, hard goods and wet; bought and sold, wholesale and retail, and were ready to change their occupation and embark in some new nondescript undertaking after two minutes' consideration.

As we have said, there were no homes at this period in San Francisco, and time was too precious for anyone to stay within doors to cook victuals. Consequently an immense majority of the people took their meals at restaurants, boarding-houses and hotels —the number of which was naturally therefore very great; while many lodged as well as boarded at such places. Many of these were indeed miserable hovels, which showed only bad fare and worse attendance, dirt, discomfort and high prices. A few others again were of a superior class; but, of course, still higher charges had to be made for the better accommodation. At night, they lay from half a dozen to two score in a room, on the floor, in rows of cots, or contracted and filthy bunks fastened to the weather-boards from floor to ceiling, in which were immense swarms of fleas and other troublesome vermin. At some lodging-houses and hotels, every superficial inch—on

Miner's Foundry and the Selby Shot Tower (they actually made "shot" or ammunition for guns) First Street, near Howard, San Francisco, California, 1860s.

Library of Congress, Lawrence & Houseworth Collection

[Regarding the Vigilance Committee] The legal authorities, with numerous practising lawyers in their train, meanwhile "fretted and fumed" at thus losing their own proper business; and denounced in angry language the sweeping action of the committee. Those personages did not deny the good result of this action, nor did they disguise the alarming increase of crime and the inability of the regular tribunals to cope with it; but still they harped upon the illegality, — the illegality of the whole proceedings. Illegality truly! People were abused, robbed and murdered on all sides, their houses set in flames, and their goods consumed or stolen, and yet they were to be forbidden the only remedy in their power, because form was to be observed, while criminals escaped! The reproaches of mere lawyers were disregarded, and the work of purification went on.

Portsmouth Square in the 1860s. It's now part of Chinatown, in San Francisco.

On Tuesday, October 29, 1850, a great celebration was held in honor of the admission of California as one of the states of the American Union.

No effort has been spared to make it a success and two thousand persons have subscribed for the dinner and ball at one hundred francs each. Various organizations assembled, banners in hand, and formed a large procession which was to parade the streets.

At ten that morning the parade started. In it were groups of pioneers, Freemasons, and many other fraternities, each wearing their own insignia and walking in groups. There were also groups of Chinese, sailors, firemen, soldiers, ministers, and the officials of the city. At regular intervals marched bands of musicians.

The parade was long and colorful. At the end came a colossal chariot drawn by six horses. On it sat thirty children dressed in blue trousers with belts and shirts of white wool, carrying shields or escutcheons, signifying the thirty states of the Union. All wore liberty bonnets — not, however, as a sign of such liberty and lawlessness as we find out here.

Ernest de Massey, 1850

floor, tables, benches, shelves, and beds, was covered with a portion of weary humanity.

To vary amusements, occasionally a fancy-dress ball or masquerade would be announced at high prices. There the most extraordinary scenes were exhibited, as might have been expected where the actors and dancers were chiefly hot-headed young men, flush of money and half frantic with excitement, and lewd girls freed from the necessity of all moral restraints.

Gambling was a peculiar feature of San Francisco at this time. It was the amusement—the grand occupation of many classes—apparently the life and soul of the place. There were hundreds of gambling saloons in the town. The bar-room of every hotel and public house presented its tables to attract the idle, the eager and covetous. Monte, faro, roulette, rondo, rouge et noir and vingt-un, were the games chiefly played. In the larger saloons, beautiful and well-dressed women dealt out the cards or turned the roulette wheel, while lascivious pictures hung on the walls.

The sums staked were occasionally enormous. One evening sixteen thousand dollars' worth of gold dust was laid upon a faro table as a bet. This was lost by the keeper of the table, who counted out the money to the winner without a murmur, and continued his business with a cheerful countenance, and apparently with as good spirits as though he had incurred no more than an ordinary loss. The professional gamblers, who paid great rents for the right of placing their tables in these saloons, made large fortunes by the business. Their tables were piled with heaps of gold and silver coin, with bags of gold dust, and lumps of the pure metal, to tempt the gazer. The sight of such treasures, the occasional success of players, the music, the bustle, heat, drink, greed and deviltry, all combined to encourage play to an extent limited only by the great wealth of the community. Judges and clergymen, physicians and advocates, merchants and clerks, contractors, shopkeepers, tradesmen, mechanics and laborers, miners and farmers, all adventurers in their kind——every one elbowed his way to the gaming-table, and unblushingly threw down his golden or silver stake. The whole of the eastern side of Portsmouth Square, three-fourths of the northern, and a portion of the southern sides were occupied by buildings specially devoted to gambling.

We have occasionally alluded to the desertion of seamen. At the time of which we write there were between three and four hundred large square-rigged vessels lying in the bay, unable to leave on account of want of hands. Many of these vessels never got away, but, in a few years afterwards, rotted and tumbled to

Once, I took my place in a sort of long, post-office single file of miners, to patiently await my chance to peep through a crack in the cabin and get a sight of the splendid new sensation —a genuine, live Woman! And at the end of half of an hour my turn came, and I put my eye to the crack, and there she was, with one arm akimbo, and tossing flap-jacks in a frying-pan with the other.

And she was one hundred and sixty-five years old, and hadn't a tooth in her head.

[Note : Being in calmer mood, now, I voluntarily knock off a hundred from that. —M.T.]

Mark Twain, 1872

The "America" Riverboat, deep in mud, 1860s.

Steve Crandell Collection, Restoration by Steve Crandell

I enjoyed my first earthquake. It was one which was long called the "great" earthquake, and is doubtless so distinguished till this day. It was just after noon, on a bright October day. I was coming down Third street. The only objects in motion anywhere in sight in that thickly built and populous quarter, were a man in a buggy behind me, and a street car wending slowly up the cross street. Otherwise, all was solitude and a Sabbath stillness. As I turned the corner, around a frame house, there was a great rattle and jar, and it occurred to me that here was an item! —no doubt a fight in that house. Before I could turn and seek the door, there came a really terrific shock; the ground seemed to roll under me in waves, interrupted by a violent joggling up and down, and there was a heavy grinding noise as of brick houses rubbing together. I fell up against the frame house and hurt my elbow. I knew what it was, now, and from mere reportorial instinct, nothing else, took out my watch and noted the time of day; at that moment a third and still severer shock came, and as I reeled about on the pavement trying to keep my footing, I saw a sight! The entire front of a tall four-story brick building in Third street sprung

Continued in far right column

Thousands of homes and commercial buildings were being erected to handle the population boom. Often times earthquakes and fires would bring the primitive structures down once again. Thus, logging nearby redwood forests and the pine and hardwood forests in the valley and Sierras bacame a booming business.

pieces where they were moored. As stores and dwelling houses were much needed, a considerable number of the deserted ships were drawn high on the beach, and fast imbedded in deep mud, where they were converted into warehouses and lodgings for the wants of the crowded population. When subsequently the town was extended over the mud flat of the bay, these ships were for ever closed in by numberless streets and regularly built houses both of brick and frame.

Rents were correspondingly enormous. Three thousand dollars a month, in advance, was charged for a single store, of limited dimensions, and rudely constructed of rough boards. A certain two story frame building, known as the "Parker House," and situated on Kearny street, paid its owners one hundred and twenty thousand dollars a year in rents. The "El Dorado," a gambling saloon, which adjoined the Parker House on the right, at the corner of Washington street, and which was only a canvas tent of moderate size, brought at the rate of forty thousand dollars per annum. The interest of borrowed money was rated by the same scale. From eight to fifteen per cent per month, with the addition of real security, was regularly given, in advance, for the use of money. And people paid these enormous wages, rents and interests; and still made fortunes to themselves! Real estate, that but a few years before was of little more worth than an old song, now brought amazing prices. From plain twelve dollars for fifty-vara lots, prices gradually rose to hundreds, thousands and tens of thousands of dollars; so that large holders of such properties became on a sudden millionnaires. The holder of every office in the State and municipality was paid generously. There was no niggardliness in such things. A religious body, whose clergymen are seldom in the habit of receiving extravagant salaries, took the support of their minister on themselves, and voted him the princely allowance of ten thousand dollars per annum!

The main-spring of all this bustle and money-making trade was the gold mining. Consider, therefore, the mightily enhanced prices of every article at the diggings! Gold dust paid for all foreign supplies, and filled the pockets of every active and shrewd man besides. Millions' worth of pure gold, in lumps and dust, reached San Francisco every month. The greater portion was forwarded to the Atlantic States. Future generations will see California a rich and prosperous country independently altogether of her mineral wealth; but in those early days it was the placers alone that made, and which are still making it what it appears. All honor then to the sturdy and independent digger, whose labors are peopling the country, cultivating the fields, building cities, making roads, covering the ocean and the bays and the rivers of the land with steamers and great ships, and conferring riches and happiness not only on the growing popu-

San Francisco's waterfront has always been a hubbub of activity.

Steve Crandell Collection, Restoration by Steve Crandell

Continued from far left column

outward like a door and fell sprawling across the street, raising a dust like a great volume of smoke! And here came the buggy —overboard went the man, and in less time than I can tell it the vehicle was distributed in small fragments along three hundred yards of street.

One could have fancied that somebody had fired a charge of chair-rounds and rags down the thoroughfare. The street car had stopped, the horses were rearing and plunging, the passengers were pouring out at both ends, and one fat man had crashed half way through a glass window on one side of the car, got wedged fast and was squirming and screaming like an impaled madman.

Every door, of every house, as far as the eye could reach, was vomiting a stream of human beings; and almost before one could execute a wink and begin another, there was a massed multitude of people stretching in endless procession down every street my position commanded. Never was solemn solitude turned into teeming life quicker.

Mark Twain, 1872

The Oakland Ferry and Steamer Washoe in San Francisco, 1860s.

 Mark Twain, Bret Harte, Prentice Mulford and Dinsmore arrived later, although it is generally believed by archaeologists that Mark Twain started for California immediately after the deluge, but owing to snags in the Mississippi River and scientific researches en route, did not actually arrive in California until A. D. 1852. The first opening that occurred after his arrival in San Francisco was caused by an earthquake. This event so exasperated Mark, that he immediately laid in a box of pipes, a barrel of smoking tobacco and a few kegs of lager as small stores, and sailed direct for the Sandwich Islands, where for several years he hobnobbed with King Kamehameha, and played "Jumping Frog of the Calaveras," for the amusement of Prince Kalakaua and other sprigs of Kanaka royalty.

Samuel C. Upham, 1853-1854

lation of California itself, that shall hereafter be numbered by millions instead of the present hundreds of thousands.

While labor was so well paid at this period, in San Francisco, it is a melancholy fact that there was much destitution, sickness, and even death by want and exposure in the place. Many of the immigrants had landed in a sickly and emaciated state, ill of scurvy and other diseases which their long voyage and hardships had produced; and such people could not work. Others had miscalculated their own powers and inclinations, and the nature of the country they had come to, and were either ashamed or unable to perform honest labor. Disappointed diggers, returning from the mines with broken constitutions, swelled the destitute population. They probably lived in miserable habitations, sleeping often upon the bare earth. Around them were bustle and lucrative pursuits, while they alone seemed neglected. Then they lost heart, pined, took sick and died, cursing the country and its gold, and the foolish fancies that had led them to it. Many committed suicide in the utter prostration of physical strength, in feebleness or disease of mind and absolute despair.

The every-day aspect of the plaza and streets was of the most curious and interesting kind. Take the plaza, on a fine day, for a picture of the people. All races were represented. There were hordes of long pig-tailed, blear-eyed, rank-smelling

Chinese, with their yellow faces and blue garbs; single dandy black fellows, of nearly as bad an odor, who strutted as only the negro can strut, in holiday clothes and clean white shirt; a few diminutive fiery eyed Malays, from the western archipelago, and some handsome Kanakas from the Sandwich Islands; jet-black, straight featured, Abyssinians; hideously tattooed New Zealanders; Feejee sailors and even the secluded Japanese, short, thick, clumsy, ever-bowing, jacketed fellows; the people of the many races of Hindoo land; Russians with furs and sables; a stray, turbaned, stately Turk or two, and occasionally a half naked shivering Indian; multitudes of the Spanish race from every country of the Americas, partly pure, partly crossed with red blood, Chilians, Peruvians and Mexicans, all with different shades of the same swarthy complexion, black-eyed and well-featured, proud of their beards and moustaches, their grease, dirt, and eternal gaudy serapes or darker cloaks; Spaniards from the mother country, more dignified, polite and pompous than even their old colonial brethren; "greasers," too, like them; great numbers of tall, goat-chinned, smooth-cheeked, oily-locked, lank-visaged, tobacco-chewing, large-limbed and featured, rough, care-worn, careless Americans from every State of the Union, dressed independently in every variety of garb, not caring a fig what people thought of them, but determined to "do the thing handsomely," and "go ahead;" fat, conceited, comfortable Englishmen, who pretended to compete in shrewdness

Giant redwoods, which may have taken 2,000-3,000 years to grow, fell with such regularity that today only 4% of the ancient trees survive.

California State Archives

After hanging [James Stuart] a few seconds his hat fell off, and a slight breeze stirred and gently waved his hair. This was a sorry spectacle — a human being dying like a dog, while thousands of erring mortals, whose wickedness only had not yet been found out, looked on and applauded! But necessity, which dared not trust itself to feelings of compassion, commanded the deed, and unprofitable sentiment sunk abashed. Reason loudly declared — *So perish every villain who would hurt his neighbor*! and all the people said *Amen!*

Music Day at Golden Gate Park, 1879.

I fell in love with the most cordial and sociable city in the Union. After the sage-brush and alkali deserts of Washoe, San Francisco was Paradise to me. I lived at the best hotel, exhibited my clothes in the most conspicuous places, infested the opera, and learned to seem enraptured with music which oftener afflicted my ignorant ear than enchanted it, if I had had the vulgar honesty to confess it. However, I suppose I was not greatly worse than the most of my countrymen in that. I had longed to be a butterfly, and I was one at last. I attended private parties in sumptuous evening dress, simpered and aired my graces like a born beau, and polked and schottisched with a step peculiar to myself — and the kangaroo.

Mark Twain, 1872

with the subtle Yankee-as if it were not the "manifest destiny" of Jonathan, every where, but especially on his own ground, to outshine John! Then there were bands of gay, easy-principled, philosophical Germans, Italians and Frenchmen of every cut and figure, their faces covered with hair, and with strange habiliments on their persons, and among whom might be particularly remarked numbers of thick-lipped, hook-nosed, ox-eyed, cunning, oily Jews. Among this vast motley crowd scarcely could two hats be found alike in material, size and shape; scarcely could two men be found otherwise dressed alike. The long-legged boot, with every variety of colored top, the buckled-up trousers, serapes or cloaks, pea-jackets and broad-brimmed or slouched hats and glazed caps, were perhaps the commonest articles of dress. The fortunate miner with his dirty garments and hirsute face, could be readily distinguished from all others. He cared not to dress or cleanse himself properly, till the bars and gambling saloons had been duly visited, and his hard won gains were spent. Then did he shake, shave and wash himself, and start again for the golden placers.

The eye was delighted with the varieties of costume, and more readily distinguished the wearers; while the ear was only confounded with the babble of unknown, and to it harsh, guttural and meaningless sounds which flowed from every mouth, and where all alike talked loudly, and many furiously gesticulated.

Every body, of course, was anxiously expecting letters from home; and every body hastened to look after them. So anxious were many to receive their epistles, that they posted themselves in the evening of one day to be early at the window on the morning of the next, standing all night in the mud, with a heavy rain pouring down upon their heads. Sometimes people would employ and handsomely pay others to preserve places for them, which they would occupy, in room of their assistants, when they were approaching the loop-holes where the delivery clerks stood. Ten and twenty dollars were often paid for accommodation in this way.

Turning from these busy scenes and ascending a neighboring height, the wearied spectator beheld one of the most peaceful prospects and pleasant sights of the world. Beyond the narrow limits of the town were the calm waters of the bay, on which floated, swan-like, hundreds of trim and well-proportioned ships, all motionless, and deserted by their crews. Farther out was the high lying island of Yerba Buena, green to the summit. Beyond it lay the mountains of Contra Costa, likewise arrayed in verdant robes, on the very tops of which flourished groups of huge redwood trees; while far in the distance towered the gray head of Monte Diablo. The eye wandered to the northern and southern extremities of the bay, and still gazed on green hills,

An Englishman called Frederick J. Roe, who had killed a blacksmith named Myers because he was trying to protect a young miner whom Roe and three other gamblers assaulted when he refused to gamble, was arrested by a mob who pronounced them guilty despite the efforts of the authorities who called for a trial by jury. Roe was finally tried and sentenced to be hung.

The mob then raided the prison, got possession of the prisoner, and led him out to be executed. This proceeding was sanctioned by nearly five thousand citizens. A gallows was improvised in a tree and the condemned man, supported by several ministers, declared he had yielded to a sudden impulse. Then he asked for a glass of water, and murmuring these words, "God have mercy on my soul," he was hung.

Ernest de Massey,
1850-51

The first Cliff House was a modest structure built in 1863 (see page 68). On Christmas Day 1894, it was destroyed by fire. Owner, Adolph Sutro spent $50,000 in 1896 to rebuild the Cliff House in grandiose style (below). This building survived the 1906 earthquake only to perish in a fire in 1907.

Steve Crandell Collection, Restoration by Steve Crandell

By broad stairways we reach the baths. The length of the baths is 4,995 feet; amount of glass used, 100,000 superficial feet; lumber, 3,500,000 feet, etc., etc. I will not weary you with figures; sight alone can give a comprehensive idea of their construction. A restaurant with capacity for 1,000 people is under this roof. While watching the bathers in the six various tanks we were treated to an historical play by Japanese performers, gorgeously attired in red and gilt costumes, and the music—oh! that noise still rings in my ears; it sounded about like the noise produced from pounding on big iron kettles; we really got more noise than our money's worth and left. Golden Gate Park lies in the western part of the city, reclaimed from the sand dunes, and covers 1,013 acres, being three miles long and one-half mile wide. Its conservatory, deer park, aviary, children's playhouse and artificial lake and waterfall, combined with an excellent museum, were enough to interest us for an entire day.

Loraine Immen, 1896

Sutro Baths opened in 1896 to a dazzled public at an estimated cost of over $1,000,000. Initially, San Franciscans streamed to the baths on one of three railroads connected to the city. The baths were not commercially successful and in 1937 the property was turned into a skating rink, which also failed. The structure burned down in 1966.

smooth waters and picturesque islands. It turned oceanward, and saw the Golden Gate studded with deep laden ships inward bound. The grand northern shores of the strait rose boldly and brokenly to the height of nearly three thousand feet, while the lower coast opposite was equally beautiful from the freshness of its fields and bushes, in the midst of which, and in the most beautiful spot embraced in the entire view, quietly nestles the presidio, now the solitary habitation of a small detachment of United States soldiery. The great Pacific might be dimly seen beneath the dense veil of mist that hung miles out at sea opposite the Gate. Overhead was a sky as blue and as beautiful as imagination could picture; the air was fresh and balmy; the earth beneath one's feet, soft and fragrant with new herbage and flowering shrubs; while the life-giving sun shed over all its own radiance and joy. All was clear and sharp-defined; all was tranquil and motionless, except the flight of innumerable white and gray-winged gulls, that soared and fluttered among the deserted shipping in the cove before the town.

The New World was a 525 ton steamer costing $150,000. The vessel was owned by The California Steam Navigation Company. Captain Hutchins was at the helm of this extraordinary vessel touted to have "unsurpassed accommodations, unequaled speed, and for safety no rivals." This photograph is the oldest known photo taken in 1850 of Sacramento.

Chapter 5: Sacramento

The first survey of the plat of Sacramento was made in December, 1848. Previous to the year 1844, Sutter's Fort was the principal trading-post in Upper California, and in that year Captain Sutter and others at the Fort determined to layout and build a town on the river bank, three miles below, which was to be called Sutter. The first house was erected by Captain Sutter himself. Sutterville continued to flourish unrivalled until about the time gold was discovered.

Shortly after the great discovery at Sutter's Mill, there were a number of stores located at the Fort, and an immense business was at once created at that point. The first of these mercantile establishments belonged to C. C. Smith & Co., in

At four P.M. on board the "New World" steamer for Sacramento, en route to the mountains. A great crowd on board, smoking and spitting everywhere—one cannot walk in the saloon without kicking over "spittoons," as the receiver is called, the very sight of which invites a discharge from an American mouth."

Sir Henry Vere Huntley, (1852)

Sutter's Fort, 1839-1849 — For all of its fame, Sutter's Fort had a short life. Once a thriving business center with a variety of shops to service pioneers, it was abandoned when all the tenants left for the gold fields. A few brave souls explore the empty remains of the central building in the 1860s.

The natural tendency of society, when left uncurbed by legal regulations, is toward lawlessness. So it was in the early days of California. The population in the year 1848, and the greater part of 1849, was composed of the honest and intelligent element of the eastern cities and States. But the next tide that flowed in threw upon our shores the refuse material from the larger cities on the Atlantic side of the continent, and a horde of discharged convicts from Australian Colonies. The change in society was apparent immediately; murders, robberies, and crimes of every description became every day occurrences.

which Sam Brannan was a partner. This one was started a few months before the opening of the mines, and on its counter the first exchange of gold-dust for storegoods took place.

At this time (1849) the building on the inside of Sutter's Fort was occupied by Rufus Hitchcock, the upper story being used as a boarding house. The front room below was used for drinking and gambling purposes. The bar was kept open night and day. If a customer had any coin, which was not often, the price of a drink was fifty cents; but in most cases he opened his purse and the bar-keeper took a pinch of gold dust, the extent of the pinch being regulated by the quality and quantity of the liquor consumed.

By summer all business was transferred to the embarcadero, which became the life of Sacramento.

John S. Fowler had pretty much a monopoly of freighting to the mines, which was done by means of ox-teams. He paid his teamsters from $200 to $250 a month. In the winter of 1848-9 the roads to the mines were nearly impassable. Freight from the Fort to Coloma was one dollar a pound-$2,000 per ton. Even at that price it was impossible to transport the necessaries rapidly enough to prevent serious apprehensions of famine in the remoter mining districts.

Hensley & Reading had erected a frame building in Sacramento, on the corner of I and Front streets, the first frame house in the new city. Soon after this, Mr. Ingersoll put up a structure, half canvas and half frame, between J and K, on Front street, and Mr. Stewart had a canvas house on the bank of the river, between I and J, which was opened as a tavern, or primitive hotel. In February, 1849, Sam Brannan built a frame storehouse on the corner of J and Front streets, which was soon succeeded by another belonging to Priest, Lee & Co., on the corner of J and Second, and two stylish log houses were directly after erected by Mr. Gillespie and Dr. Carpenter.

On the first of April, 1849, the number of inhabitants at the Fort and in the city did not exceed one hundred and fifty. This committee provided for the election of one Alcalde and a Sheriff, to have jurisdiction from the Coast Range to the Sierra Nevada, and throughout the length of the Sacramento Valley. And so was constituted the first American judiciary in Northern California, under a sturdy oak on the banks of the Sacramento.

From February until June 1849, there was a steady course of improvement, the immigration coming by sea, and, as yet, in not very great numbers. The political and social condition was anomalous; there was no law or system of government, and yet there was no actual disorder or discord among the free inhabitants. "The old pioneers," says Morse, constituted at that time but a small and insignificant community; and whilst they were fully impressed with the idea of the profusion of riches that sur-

Nov 29 — when we left the Ocean steamer we were let down by a rope into the small Boat and rowed by the natives as far as the Boat could for shoal water and then carried a shore in the Natives Arms and set on dry sand once while crossing the Land on the Mules we came to a river, the bank on the river was so steep that we had to be carried acrost by the stoutest gentleman the Natives leading our mules acrost and then sat on our mules again to go in a foot path through Bushes and through mudholes. Our saddles had a Horn on the back and on the front. I had all that I could do to hold on with both hands to keep from falling off. You can judge whether you would enjoy such a ride or not.

Unknown Pioneer Woman

Prison Barge on Sacramento River, 1850 — Formerly a seagoing bark, the La Grange is moored on the Sacramento River opposite H Street. Retrofitted with the gangly structure on the top, this barge served as the second Sacramento County prison from 1850 until it sank in 1859.

A view of the levee at Sacramento from the deck of the "Capitol," a 1,625 ton steamer built in 1866 that carried passengers between Sacramento & San Francisco.

Chandler bought a buggy wagon and harness and I hitched our riding horses to it and rode home, 140 miles, in three days and a half. I have been the whole length of the Sacramento valley, from Shasta to the Bay, this trip. I went on the cars from Sacramento to Vallejo, a new route and from there by boat to San Francisco in four hours. Soon the railroad will be extended the whole length of the valley. To go to White Pine I shall go to Sacramento and take the Central Pacific R. R. over the mountains to a town called Elko, 480 miles.

*Franklin A. Buck,
Red Bluff,
March 19th, 1869*

rounded them, they had not as yet a conception of the convulsive throes and conflicts of passion to which a pursuit of gold must inevitably lead."

Trading at that time yielded an enormous profit. Fifty per cent covered the expense of transportation from San Francisco, yet the Sacramento sales averaged two hundred per cent profit above the cost of goods in San Francisco. In addition to this, another large profit was derived from the purchase of gold dust, which, although the chief currency of the district, had not been adjusted to any fixed standard. The scale of valuation, in the payment for goods, ranged at first from eight to sixteen dollars per ounce. Clerks in stores were paid from three to five hundred dollars a month, and could hardly be retained at that. An immense trade sprang up between Sacramento and the mines. A constant change of purchasers was taking place, yet such was the prevailing spirit of honesty that neither goods nor gold-dust were watched with any degree of vigilance or anxiety. "Miners came to town freighted with bags of gold, which they stored away as indifferently as they did their hats and boots."

In June, immigrants by water began to arrive in thousands, on their way to the mines. Sacramento was the fitting-out place for all of them. In June an overwhelming business was in progress. The business of transportation from San Francisco became a source of enormous profit, and every craft that could float was pressed into the service. Schooners of fifty to one hundred and fifty tons burden commanded incredible prices, while fine merchant ships lying at San Francisco, and deserted by their crews, were rotting in inaction. The cost of passage from San Francisco to Sacramento was from $16 to $25, with freights at corresponding rates. On the 26th of June, the city numbered one hundred houses, including the City Hotel, on Front street, between I and J, which was said to have cost $100,000. Every sort of material that could be used in the construction of tents and houses, and stores rose to enormous value. Muslin, calico, canvas, old sails, logs, boards, zinc, tin, and old boxes, became almost priceless commodities.

As was common everywhere at that early day, public gambling became a leading and absorbing feature of the city. When merchants, bankers, and corporations would hazard nothing in architectural ornament, gamesters were erecting magnificent

On the 4th of July, 1849, a grand ball was given at the City Hotel, the then headquarters of Sacramento style and fashion. Great efforts were made to have the event on a magnificent scale, and money was spent with great prodigality. The surrounding country was scoured far and wide for ladies to grace the occasion, and the inhabitants of every ranch, log-cabin, tent, and wagon-bed were canvassed for a contribution of lady-recruits, eighteen of whom were eventually got together in the ball-room.

Tickets of admission to the ball were fixed at the moderate price of thirty-two dollars; gentlemen were required to have swallow-tail coats and white vests.

"Annie, git yer gun!" Accustomed to having to protect themselves, it was not uncommon for every pioneer family member to be armed.

Steve Crandell Collection, Restoration by Steve Crandell

1864 — The Yosemite was one of hundreds of steamers and other vessels that served Sacramento and San Francisco in their early years.

It was a wild, free, disorderly, grotesque society! Men — only swarming hosts of stalwart men — nothing juvenile, nothing feminine, visible anywhere!

Mark Twain, 1872

saloons at enormous cost. The first place of public gaming was on J street, between Second and Third. A few poles stuck in the ground, and covered with a wind-sail, constituted this first gaming rendezvous, which acquired the appropriate name of 'Stinking Tent.' Hubbard put up the famous round tent, which stood first on J street, between First and Second, and afterwards on Front, between I and J. This tent covered an area of fifty feet diameter; good music, a gorgeously decorated bar, and a gallery of obscene pictures being the chief attractions. Every species of gambling was here carried on in its most seductive aspect. Coin not being available for betting purposes, the players deposited their bags of gold-dust with the gamekeepers, and drew there from, generally until all was gone. Then they went back to the mines to dig for more.

The gambling of this time was often on a stupendous scale. Every saloon was crowded, and every table blockaded by an eager crowd of gamesters.

The bank of the river was piled with merchandise and immigrants' goods, and the facilities for storage were wholly inadequate for the great quantities arriving every day. The chief business was in miners' supplies. Lumber was scarcely to be had at fifty cents and a dollar a square foot. Teaming and packing goods to the mines was a loading business, and a source of enormous revenue. In December, fifty dollars a hundred was charged for hauling goods from Sacramento to Mormon Island and Auburn.

Nine-tenths of the adventurers arriving in San Francisco made their way to Sacramento as soon as possible, where they arrived, many of them sick, debilitated, and almost penniless. "Hence," says Morse, "from Cape Horn, from all the Isthmus routes, from Asiatic sea-ports, and from the Pacific Islands, men in the most impoverished health were converging at Sacramento; at the same time the scurvy ridden subjects of the ocean began to concentrate here. And there was another more terrible train of scorbutic sufferers coming from the overland roads. From all these sources, Sacramento became a perfect lazar-house of disease, suffering and death - when sickness came, and men began to be dependent upon each other, then it was that the channels of benevolence were found to be dry, and the very fountains of human sympathy sealed up by the most impenetrable selfishness.

There was a hospital at the Fort, but the demands for board and treatment were so exorbitant that but few could afford to go there. Other hospitals were subsequently established,

The law moved promptly and efficiently. In February, 1851, Frederick J. Roe murdered Charles H. Myers, apparently unprovoked. For this he was hung by the citizens, February 24, 1851, to a tree on Sixth street, between K and L streets.

Steve Crandell Collection, Restoration by Steve Crandell

Hanging of the Ruggles Brothers for the murder of a stage driver, 1860s

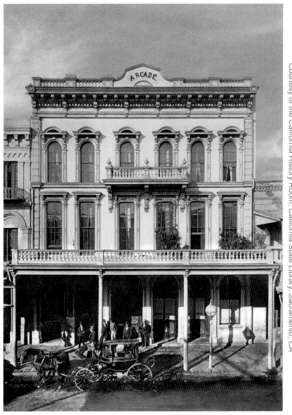

Between fires and floods, most of the oldest hotels of Sacramento were destroyed before they were ever photographed. The Arcade Hotel is shown here in 1875.

The drinking and gambling saloons abound; the first holds its ascendancy, the latter are certainly retrograding. The hotels are extremely bad, the bed-rooms nearly all two beds in them; in many, a total absence of any furniture necessary for the night, and none other, beyond a jug of water and a basin, with a towel fourteen inches square—I measured the towel in my room.

Sir Henry Vere Huntley, 1856.

which somewhat reduced the charges, but still the rates were too dear to be afforded by more than two-tenths of the sick.

On the 23d of September, the first rains came. No adequate preparation had been made for shelter from the weather, and the miseries of the sick and destitute were increased to an indescribable degree.

THE FIRST HOTEL. John S. Fowler and Samuel Brannan built the first hotel in Sacramento City, and became its proprietors. It was situated on Front street, north of J, and was afterwards called the Hotel de France. It was a two-story building, of thirty feet front, and was originally built by Sutter for a grist-mill, on the block between K and L, 28th and 29th streets, and was moved to Front street. It cost $80,000, and was opened in September, 1849, with a grand housewarming, free whisky, free wine, everything free. Whole baskets of champagne were destroyed by throwing them from the balcony and smashing them in the street.

THE SQUATTERS RIOTS. No sooner had people begun to come to Sacramento than trouble arose concerning titles to land. Nearly all of this trouble came from the fact that the titles in California were principally held by the grantees of the Mexican Government, who were protected in their rights by treaty. The settler from the East, not being conversant with this state of affairs, or aware of the great elasticity of the lines of a Mexican grant, would frequently find his home, which he had possibly spent valuable time and money in building, claimed by some one, till then only known as a large landowner, living often ten or more miles away. Again others, who knew the law, thought they could possibly succeed in getting a tract of land for themselves by taking advantage of defects in title, and a third class proposed to help themselves, and let the owner get them off if he could.

Thus, in less than one year from the commencement of immigration, we find that trouble had arisen on the vexed question of titles.

On the 7th of September, 1849, H. A. Schoolcraft petitioned the Council to remove a house built by Charles Robinson upon ground of which Schoolcraft had charge. Before this, a few men, calling themselves Squatters, had been agitating the question of Sutter's title to the land upon which the city was located. Robinson was among the first to demonstrate his earnestness, by squatting on the lot in question. It was situated on the levee, near I street, and was considered public ground. The city authorized the removal of Robinson's shanty, and it was torn down. The next day a suit was entered against the city on account of the destruction of the private property, which was decided in favor of the city. This was the beginning of the disturbances which culminated in riot and bloodshed in August succeeding.

Two wooden houses built in the 1850s on 5th Street between L & M.

Courtesy of SAMCC - Eugene Hepting Collection

By the time the levellers had reached a shanty below the foot of J street, Brannan was well warmed up to his work. In the door of the cabin stood a man evidently impressed with the great principle of the common law that every man's house is his castle. As Brannan took hold of a portion of the building with destructive intent, the owner displayed a shotgun, saying, in a solemn and sepulchral tone: "Hold on, sir! You touch this house at your peril! It's mine, and I am going to defend it!" Brannan turned to the nearest of the party, and fairly screamed out: "Warbass," cover that scoundrel, and if he raises his gun shoot h—l out of him!. The belligerent Squatter was effectually "covered," and in a few minutes his shanty had disappeared.

My Dear Wife

There has been considerable excitement and contention in this City , between the Land hold-ers, and the squatters as they are termed, though I think they are all squatters. One party pretend to hold their titles from Mr Sutter, which the other party deny his having any right or title to it The belligerants met in the streets ten days since, with firearms, and from words they proceeded to action, and one of each party was killed on the spot, also one neu-tral, an emigrant, besides wound-ing several others, among whom was the Mayor of the City. Two days after the above in attempt-ing to arrest a squatter the Sheriff was shot dead and then his possy shot two of the squatters Thus the matter stands.

E. A. Spooner
Sacramento City
Augt 25th 1850

"Colusa" was a paddle wheeler owned by the California Steam Navigation Company, 1850s.

Robinson had laid the foundation of a building where the old Water Works now stand, and projecting over the river on short piles. The regulators ripped up the floor of the obnoxious structure, and such of the piles as could be reached were pushed over. The next building attacked was a tolerably substantial one on the river bank, at the foot of I street. The vandals laid hold of a pole which supported the eaves; this, for a while, resisted their exertions, by springing back when they tugged at it. While the refractory building was under treatment, a ranchman from the country rode up, and was looking on in evident amuse-ment, when Sam Brannan — in a condition of frantic excite-ment, with a piece of manila rope around his waist, in which two revolvers were stuck-called out to the new-comer: "Get down there, - you, and lend a hand! Don't stand looking on!" The horseman slowly uncoiled his lasso from the saddle-bow and threw the looped end to Brannan, directing him to place the loop over the end of the obstinate pole, which was done. He then took a turn of the lasso round the head of his saddle, started up the mustang, and down came the pole, roof, and one side of the house, amidst the shouts of the populace. The rest of the establishment was soon disposed of.

CHOLERA. The cholera made its first appearance in Sac-ramento on the 20th of October, 1850, when an immigrant by sea was found on the levee, in the collapsing stage of the disease. The infection was brought to San Francisco on the same steamer which conveyed the intelligence of California's admission to the Union, and reached Sacramento before the city had recovered from the demoralizing effects of the Squatter riots. On the 27th, six cases were reported, and the *Times* hoped that "some precautionary measures would be taken," etc. On the 29th, twelve cases appeared; on the 30th, nineteen, and it was no longer possible to conceal the presence of the ghastly destroyer. Deaths during the past week, so far as known, 188.

On the 14th of November, the daily mortality had decreased to twelve, and on the 17th, the plague was reported as having entirely disappeared.

FLOODS. Scarcely had the hardy pioneers of California commerce established themselves upon that broad plain, where the city now stands, than the angry waves of the adjacent rivers, swollen by melting snows and falling rains, burst in upon them with mad fury.

In the evening of January 8th, 1850, a violent south-east storm came on, which swelled the Sacramento River to such an extent, that shortly after, the water began to run over the slough on I street between First and Third.

> The streets are deserted, and frequented only by the hearse. The daily mortality is about sixty.
>
> *Alta* [Newspaper]

Flood waters inundated Sacramento many times over the years.

Courtesy of SAMCC - Eugene Hepting Collection

Water, water everywhere... a common lament in the early years of Sacramento.

The trip to Sacramento proved monotonous, and the *El Dorado*, which was not built for the comfort of her passengers, was overcrowded. The night was cool, but a quiet night's rest was impossible; the banks of the Sacramento were heavily inundated... to such an extent that vehicles could not move down the streets, and residents had to use boats and canoes to carry on business.

Heinrich Lienhard, 1850

Buildings and merchandise were greatly damaged, a great quantity of goods and provisions having been swept away. Several teamsters lost from forty to fifty yoke of cattle, each, and horses and mules were drowned in corresponding numbers.

By Friday evening, January 18th, the water had receded so far as to leave several places dry on the Embarcadero, and most all of Second street; after the subsidence of the flood, great discomfort was produced by the multitude of dead cattle that were lodged everywhere about the city.

Dr. John F. Morse, has left on record the following...

"The few boats belonging to the shipping were brought into requisition in gathering up the women, children, and invalids that were scattered about in tents and canvas houses.

When hundreds of thousands of dollars in merchandise were being wrested from the merchants and traders by the sweeping currents that were running through the streets, in some places with irresistible force, no one could have found among the losers of the property a single dejected face or dejected spirit. There were no gloomy consultations, no longing looks cast upon the absconding produce, no animosities excited.

In a few weeks after the abatement of the waters, everything seemed transformed into active business and money-making. Tents and canvas houses gave place to large and commodious stores and dwellings. Business began to assume something like system; the most rapid revolutions were constantly taking place in trade; teaming became an extensive source of profit; stage lines were established, permeating every valley leading to the mines; parties and dinners, bull-fights and horse-races, theatres, Sunday schools, sewing-circles-all began an emulation for patronage.

From this beginning has arisen that mighty cordon of protective embankments which now encircles the city like a fortification, and which appears, so far as human foresight can go, to be an ample protection against the recurrence of those scenes."

For some days prior to Sunday, March 7, 1852, both the Sacramento and American Rivers had assumed threatening proportions. Continuous rains in the lowlands and heavy snow falls in the mountains produced a larger volume of water by far than their natural banks could contain, or the then insecurely built levees resist. Drowsy citizens were suddenly awakened from their slumbers by the stirring and ominous clang of the alarm

All the while that Sacramento was underwater from floods, miners continued their quest for gold. This old prospector was wandering through the foothills.

Some of the women were in tents in remote, low places, and were found standing upon beds and boxes, in water a foot deep, and which was still rising with perilous rapidity. Sick men, utterly helpless, were found floating about on cots, and, in the enfeebled tone of dissolution, were crying for help.

All the shipping and two-story houses became crowded with the unwebbed bipeds of hilarity and merriment.

Teamsters, stages, riverboats, and eventually the railroad were always in high demand. There were dozens of stage lines traveling all over Northern California. This 1880s photo is of the Courtland Stage Line.

That winter the city was visited by a flood which put nearly every part of it under water, and where our house stood the flood was several feet deep. In fact, our house was floated off its foundation. The rain had fallen in torrents for so many days continuously that a flood seemed inevitable, so father wisely found quarters for us in the loft of a barn, where, with our furniture, and hanging of sail cloths around the walls to keep out the wind that otherwise would have come through the racks, we lived quite comfortably. When the flood was the highest the water came within two feet of the loft floor. Father had a boat, and, boylike, I certainly enjoyed the situation. The barn was our domicile for the entire winter, until the waters so receded that father could replace and fix up our house.

Frank A. Leach, 1853

bell, warning them of impending catastrophe. In a few moments thereafter the streets were alive with excited men, rushing eagerly to the scene of disaster. It was found that the levee near the mouth of the American River had caved in.

Every endeavor was made to stop the breach. In spite of all, trees, houses, scows, tents everything movable-all were engulfed, and carried downward in a confused mass by the rapacious current. This material, striking the bridge at the foot of Third street with tremendous force, snapped it like a pipe-stem, and it, also, was swept away.

Cattle, pigs, and poultry of the inhabitants floated by upon a forced voyage, filling the air as they went with a very babel of mournful cries, and doleful lamentations.

From commencement to end of this flood, communication with the surrounding country was wholly cut off. Stages leaving Sacramento on the sixth instant for Auburn and Nevada, were obliged to return. Upon the following day, one was completely wrecked while endeavoring to cross the torrent at Sutter's race, the horses being saved with difficulty. Little's bridge at Coloma, the bridge at Union town, the two covered bridges at Salmon Falls, and all the bridges on the south and middle forks of the American river were destroyed. Many horses and mules were drowned while attempting to swim a deep slough near Brighton. Most of the losses were sustained by parties in the suburbs, or outside of the city. The merchants of Sacramento had, as a rule, profited by their experience of 1850, and removed their goods in time to avoid damage.

January 1, 1853, the city was again completely flooded; the water of the Sacramento rising twenty-two feet above low water mark, and two feet higher than the great flood of 1850.

March 28, 1861, the American River again rose, and quickly reached twenty feet above low water mark; this being the highest since 1853.

This, however, proved to be but the precursor of the greatest and most destructive flood of all. About eight o'clock on the morning of December 9th, 1861, it was announced that the levee upon the eastern boundary had given way, and almost immediately thereafter the waters of the American River swept in upon the city with uncontrollable fury. They came with the strength and speed of a hurricane. Well was it for the inhabitants that the break did not occur during the night, else the loss

We spent a part of Wednesday, the ninth of January, in Dr. Deal's upper room; and in the afternoon, when we came down to return to the parsonage, lo! a river came rolling down the street, meeting us. Half the city was already submerged, and the swelling flood hasted to bury the remainder.

William Taylor
Thursday,
January 10, 1850.

The State Capitol under construction, 1866. California is the 31st state and achieved statehood on September 9, 1850. Its original capitol was in San Jose, then Vallejo and on to Benicia. Sacramento became the capitol in 1854, but it temporarily moved to San Francisco from January to May, 1862 due to flooding in Sacramento. Construction on the capitol building began in 1860. It was completed in 1874 at a cost of $1,000,000.

When floods didn't keep them in 'dry dock' The Sacramento Stage Line, was one of many, that did a brisk business in its day.

A number of persons obtained boats from the Front street levee under pretence of rescuing those who were in imminent danger of drowning, and then took advantage of their extremity to extort money from the sufferers. One man had placed his wife on the roof of a house that was already tottering to its fall, and was obliged to pay one of these pirates seventy-five dollars in gold before he could take her to a place of safety.

of life must have been fearful. Within one hour from the first alarm, many persons living east of Eleventh street were surrounded by water, in imminent danger of their lives, and their calls for assistance were heart-rendering in the extreme. There was now a general movement among stock-owners. Horses, mules, cattle, hogs, and sheep were driven in great numbers across the Yolo bridge, and down the levee toward Sutterville. By eleven o'clock the water had attained such a depth at Fifth and Sixth streets, north of the railroad, that a large number of houses were overturned, and set afloat. Clinging to the doors and windows of these, women and children shrieked loudly for help. The inmates of one story residences generally deserted them, while those who occupied two-story buildings, carried all movable articles up stairs.

During that night several houses floated past upon the river, and female voices were heard within them, shrieking vainly for assistance. Two sections of Lisle's bridge across the American were swept away, but lodged against the Sacramento bridge, and were there secured.

During the life and death struggle in that portion of the city where the flood first spent its violence. Inside a house a man stood up to his chin in water, praying a passing boatman to relieve him. The boatman demanded fifteen dollars fare. The man answered that he had no money.

"Then," said the unfeeling wretch, "I'll leave you to drown." And leave him he did, but fortunately the sufferer was soon afterward rescued by a boat without charge.

NAVIGATION. The earliest navigation of the Sacramento River, of which we have any record, was in the year 1839. There may have been voyagers on the river before that date, but they left no record of their exploits, and the world is none the wiser for their bravery. The first white navigator of the Sacramento River was the famous Captain Sutter.

A correspondent, speaking of the first steam navigation of the river, says: "I made the first and only trip on Captain William A. Leidesdorff's little Russian steamer from San Francisco to New Helvetia. She had no name, but has since been called the *Sitka*.

"The day after her arrival from the Sacramento she was sunk by a south-easter in what is now Battery street. We left San Francisco on the 28th of November, 1847, and arrived at New Helvetia December 4th-six' days and seven hours out.

The Victor was a 272 ton steamer. It cost $25,000, and served the Sacramento to Marysville route, making its first trip down the river on August 13, 1859.

Library of Congress, Lawrence & Houseworth Collection

From a high mountain, from which I had an extended view, I estimated that at least one quarter of this Earthly Paradise, this charming and fertile Valley (oh!) was under water. Hundreds of cattle and mules were drowned and floated down to rejoice with the aromatic scent of their putrid carcasses the refined olfactory nerves of the citizens of Sacramento and other towns springing up on the River, and the loss of property in Sacramento City by the overflow has been very great.

Alonzo Delano's Sacramento City, March 2, 1850

Chinese junk anchored below the M Street Bridge. The ship arrived from Shanghai via Victoria B.C. Note the laundry hanging on the deck.

At that time the country was the abode of savages and wild beasts. Here, in this distant and secluded dependency of imbecile Mexico, he (Sutter) determined to rear the standard of American freedom.

Samuel C. Upham, 1849

"Occasionally the *Indian Queen,* Perry McCoon, Commander, a sloop of ten tons, would make a trip in the busy season. Capt. Sutter had, also, another line running from New Helvetia to the Hock Farm, on Feather River. She was called the *White Pinnace,* an open yawl boat, rowed and poled by six nude Diggers. She run in connection with the *Yerba Buena Line*.

"The steamer *Sacramento* was brought to San Francisco in a brig. Her owners had her put together, launched July, 1849, and put under command of Captain John Van Pelt, who has the honor of being the first American Captain who went up the Sacramento River on a steamboat.

"On the first day of September, 1849, there were eight barks, eleven brigs, and seven schooners in the port of Sacramento."

"The favorite steamer *Senator,* Captain John Van Pelt, made her first appearance, November 6, 1849; the fare was only $30. The trip was made by daylight."

With the year 1850 commerce on the inland waters of California, seemed to have assumed gigantic proportions. This is no doubt accounted for when we remember the "rush" for the "gold fields." After the news of the discovery of gold had reached the East, many persons at once shipped, around the Horn, for California. These ships arrived just in time to make the "rush" of 1850.

As soon as the trade was fairly opened for the season, it was manifest that a lively competition would soon arise between the owners of the various steamers advertised for the river route. Each boat had her agents on the wharf, or levee, prior to the hour of departure; one assuring the crowd of persons of the excellence of the *McKim* over all other boats; another declaring in the most positive and emphatic manner that the *McKim* is nothing but a propeller, a "scow," or a "Junk," while the *Senator* and *New World* have unsurpassed accommodations, unequaled speed, and for safety no rivals. These truthful agents announced the time to be eight hours, but it was more frequently twelve. The fare was reduced by this competition.

The success of inland navigation was so great that its fame was almost world-wide. Sea-going men on the Atlantic coast having learned of this, were sending out steamers for this trade.

The *Queen City*, a beautiful boat, 200 feet long, nine-foot hold, and thirty-one foot beam. On her first trip she brought 919 passengers, among the number were 117 ladies.

A new company called the "Transportation," sent up the *Marlin White*, towing a very large barge. This was the first barge ever towed up by steamer, a business now largely and profitably followed. Considerable excitement was caused by the first appearance of the *Defender*, an opposition boat. On her arrival at the levee there was no place for her to land. She finally moored to the hulk *Dimon*. A few moments showed that the steamer *Pike*, also tied to the *Dimon*, was swinging into the stream. The *Defender* at once took the place of the *Pike*. It was then discov-

The Senator, built in 1849, was a 755 ton steamer that ran the route from Sacramento to San Francisco.

Steve Crandell Collection, Restoration by Steve Crandell

My Dear Wife,

I have had some success in mining during the past month, though small from what I anticipated when I last wrote you In fact this gold digging is all a lottery business, except the labor part of it. We thought we had some eight or ten hundred dollars secured at the last writing, but we have worked it out, and got only about half that amount. And now the next thing is prospecting for another place, in the bottom of every creek far and near for days, and perhaps for weeks, until a promising location is found The labor as I have previously observed is enormously hard. And I am satisfied that none but iron constitutions can endure it without injury Every years hard labor here in the mines, I believe will increase the apparent age of men generally, from five to ten years.

E. A. Spooner
California
April 21st 1850

Sailing vessels of all types used to bring goods and people to and from San Francisco, not just stopping at the Embarcadero in Sacramento as shown here, but often sailing up and down the Sacramento River to other ports.

We have concluded to run an express to Sacramento and San Francisco for letters for miners. Accordingly I went to Kennebec & Ousleys "bars" while Josiah went to Sicard & Park's "bars" and we got some 300 names to get letters for, besides some other errands, so that I went immediately.

I have just returned from below bringing some 50 letters and $300 worth of goods. I left San Francisco just after a Steamer came in from the States so that I bought 125 N York & New Orleans papers at the rate of 15 cts each. I have sold them all for 50 cts each. The postage on letters is .40 cts, but we get $1.50 each, so that the express business more than pays the expenses of the trip, and the goods that we sell can be bought for about 1/2 in San Francisco that they can in Marysville.

Stephen David Chapin
1850-1854

ered that the gangway had been boarded up, but with axes in the hands of the deck-hands, a way was soon opened, and freight and passengers put on shore without further trouble or delay. When the hour for departure drew near, a band of music on the *Defender* enticed passengers on board that boat. The band had played but a few minutes when a small stern-wheel steamer, which was paddling in the stream, commenced to blow a sharp, shrill whistle, only stopping when the band stopped playing, and resuming its shrill sound the moment the band struck up its music.

The crowd on the levee, which was by this time large, were cursing the small steamer with a vengeance. In addition to this "free concert," a man and two boys, each with Chinese gongs, were doing their best to equal the band and outdo the steam-whistle. The noise was simply outrageous. Judge Morrison was obliged to adjourn Court for the time; and all this because of an opposition boat. Such scenes were frequent during the days of lively competition.

With the year 1860 the building of favorite steamers for this river trade seems to have taken a new stride. In the early summer the steamer *Chrysopolis*, known to all people who have gone to Sacramento, was launched at San Francisco.

The year 1864 was a memorable one for Sacramento Navigation. 'Twas in this year that the famous steamer *Yosemite* was built and brought on to a route which she has traveled for so many years. Her first trip to Sacramento was made on the 29th day of May, 1864. The peer of the *Yosemite*, the *Washoe*, exploded in this same year, and the next year the *Yosemite* herself had the same bad luck.

There were 103 schooners arrived at, and departed from Sacramento City in 1867. They averaged about 40 tons each. Harbor dues collected for 1867, $12,820.78.

April first the California Steam Navigation Company made a transfer of all their steamboats, barges and other floating property to the Central Pacific Railroad Company. The boats were kept running as before the sale.

There is but little left to say, since the C. P. R. R. has had the control. Of course there have been opposition boats; they have come and gone, as it were, with the tide. As soon as an opposition boat was put on the route, the "corporation line" reduced the fare to nominally nothing, sometimes to no charge at all, and instances have been known, when they had a stubborn

Sacramento — a busy seaport in 1870.

My Dear Wife
I have some idea when I return home, of going round the horn   It is not idle curiosity that prompts the thought of this, for my views about returning with speed, are the same as formerly   But this hope of increasing, instead of diminishing the small amount of funds, is the only reason that makes me think of it if I should conclude to take this course, I shall unite with others in the purchase of a vessel, and freight her round. Vessels can be bought in Sanfrancisco, for less than one fourth of their value in the States In this case I could not be at home short of three or four months from the time of starting, which would probably be in November.

E. A. Spooner
Augt 25th 1850

The Mindora, a lumber schooner, was one of many vessels using the ports of San Francisco and Sacramento. The voracious use of lumber for the fast-growing Northern California cities kept schooners, lumber trains, and wagon trains constantly busy.

Early in 1851 the town appeared, for a time, to have been captured by the roughs, who openly proclaimed that they would do as they pleased. At the same time there appears to have been a gang of robbers, who entered houses and stores and helped themselves with great freedom. The operations of this gang were rudely disturbed by Captain J. H. Ward, March 29, 1851, who shot and killed one burglar as he was entering a window, and halted the second by shooting him in the legs.

opposition, where the Company have actually paid passengers to take passage on their boat.

The accidents which have occurred on the Sacramento river would make a long chapter, were the full particulars to be given. This we shall not attempt, but will merely mention them:

The steamers *J. Bragdon* and *Comanche* collided, on January 5, 1853, on Suisun Bay. The *Comanche* sank in ten minutes; ten lives lost, and cargo destroyed. The *Bragdon* was roughly used by the collision. The *Comanche* was raised, refitted, and put on the line again the same year.

The *R. K. Page* was" blown up" when racing with the *Gov. Dana*, on their trip to Marysville. Four lives lost.

The *Pearl* (deceitful name) was blown up, near the mouth of the American River, on her down trip from Marysville. She had on board 101 passengers. The loss of life was very great. The cause of the disaster is supposed to have been "too little water in the boiler, and too much fire in the furnace."

February 7, 1856, the steamer *Belle*, had her boiler explode, when eleven miles above Sacramento. The *General Redding*, on her down trip, happened at the scene of the accident a few minutes after its occurrence. The captain of the *Belle*, Chas. H. Houston, and twelve others were instantly killed. Major John Bidwell, and twelve or fifteen others, were more or less injured.

FIRES. On November 2, 1852, Sacramento met with her first great fire. The *Daily Union* of November 4, 1852. We quote: "That terrible destroyer which has heretofore laid in ashes every important town in this State has at last visited our fair 'City of the Plains,' and in a few brief hours swept almost every vestige of it from existence." It is impossible for us to give our readers abroad more than a brief summary of the painfully thrilling events of the past thirty hours.

"At ten minutes past eleven o'clock on Tuesday night, the appalling cry of fire was sounded, and almost the entire population rushed into the street, and at once perceived that their direst apprehensions were more than fully realized. A dense mass of smoke and flame was seen issuing from the millinery shop of Madame Lande, on the north side of J street, two doors below Fourth street, in the heart of one of the most combustible blocks in the city. The wind for the first time in many months,

1864 was a memorable year for Sacramento navigation. 'Twas in this year that the famous steamer Yosemite was built. After being withdrawn from the river trade, this popular steamer was put on the route to Vallejo and run in connection with the Sacramento train. Her first trip to Sacramento was made on the 29th day of May, 1864. The Yosemite exploded in 1865.

Steve Crandell Collection, Restoration by Steve Crandell

My Dear Wife
I have delayed writing to you till this late date in the month, with the hope that I might receive something from your hand before being compelled to write you again: But I find this to be a delusion hope, for nothing, nothing, nothing, has been the answer to all my enquiries and messages from Sanfrancisco, Sacramento, and Weaver since I have been in the country. And I know not now whether I have a friend on Earth; for I have not received a solitary line from any person since leaving Independence. The last letter recd was from yourself, and is now before me. It is dated April 8th 1849.

Believe me my Dearest one your most devoted and Affectionate Friend

E. A. Spooner
California
February 22 1850

NB Please direct all communications for me to Sacramento City, California

The name of this blood-thirsty bandit [Joaquin Murietta] is recalled, even now, with a shudder, ...when they roamed from one end of the State to the other, robbing and murdering unprotected travelers.

He was of Spanish or Mexican origin, and had a sister living in Marysville, in 1850 and 1851.

His band were partly Mexicans and partly desperadoes of other nationalities. In November, 1851, he made a raid through this region, leaving his bloody trail behind him. Within a few days, the bodies of twenty-three men who had been murdered and robbed were found. The larger portion of them indicated that the unsuspecting victim, while quietly pursuing his way on the public highway, had been lassoed from an ambuscade, dragged into the bushes, and dispatched with a knife. The whole region flew to arms; sheriffs' posses and vigilance committees scoured the country in search of the perpetrators, but they escaped to the southern part of the State.

Miller Brothers Store, 1895, run by Jacob B. and Edward Miller, whose business was stoves, tinners, and cornice makers, 1116 J Street. Paul Graf, harness maker had his business to the left at 1120 J Street.

was blowing a gale from the north, and, with the rapidity of thought the devouring element shot forth its lurid fangs, fastening upon the frail wooden tenements on either side of the burning building, and enveloping them in a sheet of fire.

"On the opposite side, the fire was checked for a time by the fire-brick block of buildings occupied by Mitchell & Co., shoe dealers; Brown, Henry & Co., wholesale dealers in dry goods; W. R. Hopkins & Co., and the upper stories by Johnson, daguerreotypist; Winans and Hyer, lawyers, and others. But the insidious foe stealthily darted upon the sheds and rookeries in the rear of this block, and soon after, this row, piled with the costliest goods, presented naught but a mass of rubbish.

On the 13th of July, 1854, occurred the second general conflagration in Sacramento's history. The alarm was rung shortly after 1 P.M. The fire started in a small frame building in the rear of Newcomb's furniture store, near the center the block bounded by J, K, Third and Fourth streets, and was caused by the upsetting of a spirit-lamp which was being used to warm a glue-pot. The flames almost immediately communicated with the kitchen of the Sacramento Hotel, and in a few moments more became a very large fire.

When the fire threatened the Court House with destruction, Governor Bigler, who had been working from the beginning, wherever Sacramento most needed a soldier, asked several bystanders to assist him in saving the furniture. The parties demurred to this on the ground that private parties could not afford to lose their property so well as the county. A full length portrait of Washington was standing against the southern wall, and, pointing to it, Bigler said See! there is the portrait of the Father of your country. Will you permit it to be destroyed?" A general rush was made and the picture saved. The Golden Eagle Hotel, a substantial brick structure, checked the fire until it was controlled.

Between twelve and one o'clock on the morning of September 6, 1872, a fire broke out in the building known as the Chinese Chapel, on the corner of Sixth and H streets. The lower story of the building was occupied as a grocery store, and the upper story as a residence by J. H. Murphy and family. When the fire was discovered it was too late to escape by the stairs, and the only alternative was to jump from the second-story window, or roast. Mrs. Murphy was instantly killed by the shock of the fall; Miss McDowell, who was visiting Mrs. Murphy, was severely injured, and, for a time, it was supposed that her injuries would also prove fatal.

RAILROADS. The project of building a railroad across the continent was first agitated by Mr. Asa Whitney, in 1846. He continued to urge the matter in Congress and out of it and was supported in his movement by such men Senators Breese, of Illinois, and Benton, of Missouri, of whom introduced a bill

At 6 P.M. while standing at the Steamboat landing, the steamer "Fashion" from San Francisco came in. When within hailing distance the Capt shouted to the assembled multitude that "San Francisco was in ashes," that "$10 000 000 worth of property was destroyed by fire on the night of May 3d." The effect produced upon that crowd was so powerful as to be worth noticing. Some shouted, some groaned, some cried, "I am ruined," some seemed completely bewildered, some ran one way & some another; but all felt that a great calamity had befallen California.[*]

Stephen Chapin David, 1851

This 1895 photo of the Visu Stables at 908 9th Street may be more than what it seems. Its signs advertise "Signs, Decorating, and Paper Hanging. Window signs offer "Pleasure Rooms." Next door is the Hope Electric Company.

The Embarcadero at Sacramento was the hub of rail, shipping and stage transportation from its inception. Photo 1864.

July 9, 1851, James Wilson, a resident of Cosumnes Township, was knocked down and robbed by four men of Sacramento in broad daylight. They were all four arrested and witnesses proved that they were the parties who had done the act. An excited crowd of about one thousand people gathered around the Station-house, and, for a time, it seemed as if the thieves would be lynched.

The Court convened, and defendants' counsel, after some demur, waiving their right to demand time, the trial proceeded.

William Robinson was tried first, and found guilty by the jury; punishment, death.

James Gibson was tried on the 15th, found guilty, and given the same sentence as Robinson.

John Thompson was also found guilty and sentenced to death.

into the Senate of the States, for a Pacific Railroad, February 7, 1849.

The first effort made in California towards the buildings of an overland road, was the formation of a company by citizens of Nevada, Placer and Sacramento counties. A line was surveyed from Sacramento City, through Folsom, Auburn, and Grass Valley, to Nevada City. This line was sixty-eight miles long, and the estimated cost of construction was $2,000,000. From Nevada City the survey was continued through the Henness Pass. The demonstration of the fact that such a route (over the Rocky mountains and the Sierra Nevadas) did exist, was left to be made by Theodore D. Judah, the Chief Engineer of the first railroad ever built in California-the Sacramento Valley Railroad. It was while engaged in building this road, from 1854-1856, that Mr. Judah became convinced of the practicability of a railroad over the Sierra Nevadas, which was the only mountain range that had heretofore been deemed impracticable.

Mr. Judah made trial surveys, or, more properly, reconnoisances over several of the supposed passes over the Sierras, at his own expense. These were simply barometrical surveys, but were sufficiently accurate to convince Mr. Judah that a road could be built, and, armed with the data thus obtained, he lost no opportunity in presenting his views and aims whenever and wherever it seemed to him that it would advance the project of a Pacific railroad.

He succeeded, through a concurrent resolution of the California Legislature of 1858.

Mr. Judah had placed his plans and estimates before a friend, Mr. James Bailey, of Sacramento. Mr. Bailey, struck by the force of these calculations, introduced Mr. Judah to Governor Stanford, Mark Hopkins and E. B. and Charles Crocker; Mr. Huntington he knew before. A meeting of the business men of Sacramento was called and the preliminary steps were taken to organize a company. The company was named The Central Pacific Railroad Company of California.

Mr. Judah went east on this mission, and this time accomplished his purpose, as was evidenced by the bill which passed Congress in July, 1862.

This bill granted a free right of way to the roads of four hundred feet wide over all Government lands on their route.

The engineering difficulties were great, and had been considered insurmountable, but the financial difficulties were also great, and undoubtedly required more labor and thought than the engineering, though of a different kind.

In 1862 the Company was granted the right of way into the City of Sacramento, and also granted the Slough or Sutter Lake. The first shovelfull of dirt thrown in the construction of the Central Pacific Railroad was in Sacramento, on the 22d

Gregory Barnes & Company, - 126/128 J Street, Sacramento, 1885

Well my Dear Wife,

here I am still at the old winter quarters, hauled up in my home-made arm chair before a little table that swings from the side of the house to have a little sociable time with Your Dear self. On this table there is a variety of things; in a little tin box about the size of one for keeping jewels, is some six or eight oz of gold dust, the labors of myself & partner for the last few days: There is a picture of a certain young Lady that seems to occupy a very prominent position here, that seems to call up many pleasing recollections of the past. It looks interesting and thoughtful as though ready to speak, but the language if any is transmitted by the look, in this manner it speaks volumes, and far exceeds the reality, who to me is mute in every particular; indeed I know not but this shadow is all I possess of what I once prized so highly.

*E. A. Spooner
California
March 2nd 1850*

Lumber was needed everywhere, and trains, like every other mode of transportation, were widely used to bring the logs, frequently out of the mountains, to the mills in the lower elevations & valley.

On May 7, 1855, Frederick Bohle, commonly known as "Dutch Fred" living a short distance from Daylor's ranch, was found dead, having been terribly cut and mangled by a his murderer. A man named William Lomax was arrested at "Our House," on Eighth street, in Sacramento, on the 10th he had been seen around the murdered man's house a few days previously. Lomax was taken to Daylor's ranch, and, on the preliminary trial, was committed by Justice Grimshaw. While awaiting an opportunity to return him to Sacramento, the neighbors of the murdered man arrived, tried Lomax, convicted him, and hung him May 14. The evidence was strong, but entirely circumstantial.

of February, 1863. Twenty miles of road each year, were completed in 1863, 1864 and 1865, thirty miles in 1866, forty-six miles in 1867, three hundred and sixty-four miles in 1868, one hundred and ninety and one-half miles in 1869; making six hundred and ninety and one-half miles from Sacramento to Promontory, where the roads met, May 10, 1869.

All of the materials, except the cross-ties, for constructing this road, including a large portion of the men employed, had to be brought from the East, via Cape Horn. Toward the latter end of the work several thousand Chinamen were employed.

The road progressed, slowly at first but more rapidly towards the close, until, on the 10th day of May, 1869, the last spike was driven, which completed the railroad connection between the Atlantic and Pacific Oceans.

The *Jupiter*, a locomotive of the Central Pacific Railroad Company, and locomotive No. 116, of the Union Pacific Railroad Company, approached from each way, and rubbed their pilots together, while bottles of champagne were passed from one to the other.

On August 20, 1870, the Western Pacific, San Joaquin Valley, California and Oregon, and San Francisco, Oakland and Alameda Railroads were all consolidated under the name of the Central Pacific Railroad.

THE WESTERN PACIFIC RAILROAD COMPANY. This Company was incorporated December 13, 1862, for the purpose of constructing a railway from San Jose, through the counties of Alameda and San Joaquin, to the City of Sacramento.

THE CALIFORNIA RAILROAD COMPANY. This Company was for some time an active competitor for the carrying trade of the State, and at one time it was thought that the intention of its owners was to construct a line of railroad to connect with the Union Pacific. This Company bought the boats and franchises of the California Steam Navigation Company, and for some time really controlled the rates of freight between Sacramento and San Francisco.

On the 28th of December, 1879, the new road via Benicia was opened, and the trains were run through to San Francisco.

SACRAMENTO VALLEY RAILROAD. This was the first railroad constructed in California. The Company was organized August 4, 1852, when ten per cent of the stock subscribed was paid in, amounting to $5000. The Company re-organized. November 9, 1854, and made immediate preparation for building the road. The first shovel-full of dirt was thrown in February, 1855, the first tie came in May, and the first vessel load of material and rolling stock arrived from Boston in June. The first work done on a railroad car in California was on this road, July

Sacramento Valley Railroad, 1869 Locomotive # 162 is on the tracks at foot of U Street, Sacramento. Behind to the right, the Opposition Steamship Line storage shed for the steamer Chin Du Wan.

There are "stages," as covered waggons are called, traversing the country for more than a hundred miles into the mountains; they are, however, most comfortless conveyances; when I have travelled by one, I will mention it more particularly.

The stage had to encounter some very soft places frequently, and two or three times "came near to miring." The last twenty miles are very mountainous, the road often so much on the incline, that the driver calls out, "Sit up to windward," and every one scrambles to the high side of the vehicle; I have seen a wheel actually off the ground, and brought to it again by "sitting to windward;" the driver lighting his cigar at the time.

Sir Henry Vere Huntley, 1856

An 1864 view of the Central Pacific's "Governor Stanford" No. 1, a wood-burning engine with men in the railroad yards on Front Street. Note the hand car at left and stacks of rails at right.

The R. R. is a great thing for the Indians. They ride free. They live around the stations and beg for two bits from the passengers. They come into town on every freight train and cut wood. The squaws wash and sell fish and dress in fine clothes but they don't get drunk and so far they are ahead of the whites.

Franklin A. Buck
April 9, 1869

4, 1855. The first rail was laid August 9, 1855, and the first train was placed on the track August 14.

On November 10, 1855, an excursion train was run to Patterson's, ten miles from Sacramento, the round trip costing one dollar. By January 1, 1856, the road was completed to Alder Creek, and on February 22 was finished to Folsom. The length of the road was twenty-two and one-half miles, and cost $1,568,500. The capital stock was $800,000—$792,000 of which were issued. The road was a very profitable one from the date of its completion. Its effect was to move the terminus of the stage and freight lines running to the northern mines to Folsom, building up quite a town at that point. At one time twenty-one different stage lines were centered at Folsom, all leaving shortly after the arrival of the train from Sacramento.

In August, 1865, the Central Pacific Company purchased the Sacramento Valley road. The short line of the Sacramento Valley road alone, declared an annual profit of nearly half a million dollars the year previous to its purchase, most of which came from the freights going to the Washoe and other mining districts.

California Central Railroad. In the Spring of 1857, a company was formed in Marysville, to build a railroad from that city to the terminus of the Sacramento Valley Railroad, at Folsom. This company was entirely independent of the Sacramento Valley Company. By 1861, the track was laid as far as Lincoln. The name was subsequently changed to the California and Oregon Railroad, and is now known as the Oregon Division of the Central Pacific Railroad.

Shortly after the completion of the Central Pacific Railroad to Roseville, the Company purchased the California Central Railroad; that portion of the road between Roseville and Folsom was abandoned; the bridge over the American River was condemned and sold in 1868.

Placerville and Sacramento Valley Railroad. This road commences at Folsom and runs to Shingle Springs, in El Dorado County, and is commonly known as the Shingle Springs road. This road was constructed in 1864 or '5.

Central Pacific Railroad Shops. The principal workshops, manufactories, and machine storehouses of the Central Pacific Railroad Company are situated in the north-western portion of the city, on a plateau, formed principally, by the Company, with earth, hauled from a point which used to be the

Turntables like this one were found all over Northern California after 1869. Once the locomotive was on the track, it was turned by "people power."

Folsom Historical Society

This is my birth day, being 18 years old. I have made another trip to San Francisco, and got quite a number of letters. As soon as I come in sight of the "bar" on my return, the miners drop their tools and run to meet me, in haste to get the letters from their dear friends at home. And those who are so unfortunate as to receive no letters, frequently rate their friends at home most severely, for neglecting so important a duty. And as they look upon their fellow-miners (who are more fortunate) reading epistles of friendships and constancy penned in the fine hand of a female, frequently a tear comes unbidden to the eye, while the heart greives at being thus forggotton by loved ones at home.

Stephen Chapin David
1850-1854

View of the Central Pacific shops looking across Sutter's Lake (China Slough) with the roundhouse at left of a cluster of buildings. 1870.

Jack Thompson, Barney Ackerman, and Charles Stewart were hung, near Sutter's Fort, April 29, 1853, for the murder of John Carroll, alias Boot Jack, February 20, 1853. These four men, and a man named Dunham, formed a gang of ruffians engaged in all sorts of villainy. They became suspicious of Carroll, and it was arranged that Dunham should kill him. This he did, Carroll being found on the levee the next morning with three shot holes in his head, either of which would have been fatal. Dunham escaped hanging by turning State's evidence.

mouth of the American River, and deposited in what is known as Sutter Lake, or China Slough. Fifteen feet was the average of the filling-in. These railroad shops are not the largest in the United States, but they are, without doubt, the most complete and best arranged. All the principal buildings are of brick, and most substantially constructed, and the machinery throughout is of the latest and most approved patterns.

The new depot erected on the Company's grounds during 1879 is by far the finest building of the kind west of Omaha. The business of Sacramento has been increasing from year to year until finally the old buildings at the foot of I street were unable to accommodate it. When the Railroad Company began to make arrangements for running trains via Benicia, they caused plans to be made for a new depot which should be able to accommodate all the passenger business likely to come to Sacramento for all time. This building is now completed on made ground, reclaimed or filled in from China Slough, between G and I, Front and Third streets.

The general style of the building is Gothic and its architectural appearance is impressive and beautiful. It consists of a central pile of buildings, a portion being two stories in hight, faced by a depot arcade or sheltered avenue, seventy feet wide and 414 feet long. This arcade contains the tracks on which the different trains enter and leave the depot. The roof of this portion is corrugated iron. The pile of buildings referred to is 164 feet long.

AMUSEMENTS. Horse racing, and bull and bear fights seem the most popular amusements.

Bull fighting is a Spanish entertainment with which man stimulates animal lust and animal rage until a bloody victim falls to the battle ground amidst the barbarous jubilation of the crowd. The rage of the bull is not stimulated here by deception, spear or fireworks, but by a bear who is chained to the front foot of the bull.

The first of these bull fights took place in the summer of 1851 in Sacramento City. It was a burning hot afternoon and the arena was shaded only by some oak trees under which the mounted spectators had gathered while most of the crowd was in the grandstand or pushing against the balustrade of the battle field. The wild bull was a large stately brown animal, young and fat, broad-browed and with sharp horns. Several bold Americans rode close by the bull and soon pushed a rider from his saddle and then with his horns ripped open the belly of a beautiful horse.

The bull stood paralyzed and the bear hung to his head like a living padlock. The bear squeezed the bull in his arms with all his strength, sunk his claws deep behind his ears and buried the bull's nose in his bloodthirsty jaws while he braced

Central Pacific Railroad's depot at Sacramento, 1879

Courtesy of the California History Room, California State Library, Sacramento, CA

In my jugdment, the management [of the Central Pacific Railroad] is to be classed among the very best. The road bed is solid and smooth. Engines large and of superior workmanship and in thorough condition. Cars built for durability and service, and well appointed for the comfort of travelers.

Particularly has the Central inaugurated a car with an admirable sleeping contrivance for the comfort of its emigrant passengers; so, that this class, traveling at about half price, can go in as much comfort as the first-class passengers. The ferry accommodations for crossing the bay from Oakland to San Francisco are unsurpassed for elegance, magnitude, strength and dispatch, by anything in the country.

At Sacramento is one of the most splendid depots and eating houses on the continent. Cars, engines, depots, work shops, offices and eating-houses are all kept scrupulously neat and clean.

Edward Dwight Holton, 1879

This 1870 Sacramento racetrack was a popular attraction. Sulkies await their race, while judges and spectators look on.

The grizzly bear of California attains to the enormous size of eleven and twelve hundred pounds; I saw a dead one that weighed one thousand, and measured the fresh foot-print of one that was nine inches across the ball. One of Capt. Sutter's men told me an amusing story of his own attempt to lasso one of the largest he had ever seen. He threw the lasso over his head, and while attempting to entangle his legs with it, the bear settled back upon his haunches, seized it with his teeth and paws, and commenced "hauling in" horse and rider. The hunter leaped from his horse and made his escape, the horse reared and pitched at a furious rate, and by breaking the lasso avoided an uncomfortable "hug" even for a horse.

Dr. William S. McCollum, 1850

his rear legs on the ground, clawing into it with them. It seemed as if he either wanted to blow out the breath of his opponent or suck his life out. That was a bear kiss! The bull emitted such a moan of pain at this that I gritted my teeth and joined him with a sigh.

The grizzly rose to his full height and swung his paw to strike the bull a rough blow. The bull deftly side-stepped and now thrust his horns into the bear's fur. No blood flowed but the bear, overcome by a panic of fear, took to flight. The chain broke and in the wink of an eye old Bruin was sitting up in the nearest oak tree. How amusing! You should have seen the speed with which those jackanapes spectators left their reserved seats.

It was pathetic to see the poor animal, completely exhausted, forced by men to fight while dying just to decide their bets. The sight became unbearable. I withdrew and mounting my horse disappeared towards the city in the growing darkness of nightfall.

Sutter Street, 1910. Lined with stores, shops, and restaurants, from its earliest days, Folsom first served a bustling community of miners. In the 1860s it was the Western terminus of the Pony Express. The Western end of the street housed the bustling shops of the Sacramento Valley Railroad.

Chapter 6: Folsom

The history of Folsom properly includes that of Negro Bar, which was the pioneer of the former place, and it is more than probable that had it not been for the fact that there was a mining camp of large proportions at Negro Bar, Folsom would have been located farther down the American Fork. Negro Bar received its name from the circumstance of negroes being the first men to do any mining at that point. This was in 1849. The Bar commences at Folsom, on the same side of the river, and runs nine-tenths of a mile down stream. Miners came flocking in from all quarters, and in 1851 there were over seven hundred people here. In the summer of 1850 the Virginia Mining Company was formed, for draining the river at this point. It took them two years to build the canal, which was intended to leave the old river bed clear for mining. The canal was used for mining the bar, by using" Long Toms." The Bar was splendid

James K. Page was executed at 8:15 A.M., on August 10th, 1883, in the jail-yard at Placerville, for the murder of an unknown man in New York ravine, near Folsom, May 10th, 1883.

Blacksmiths thrived in the 1800s and early 1900s. Making horseshoes was but one of many services they provided. From door hinges to farm implements and wagon wheel rims, virtually every metal implement needed was made by a blacksmith.

On the morning of March 27th, 1861, the stage from Placerville to Folsom met with a very serious accident, at the crossing of Deer creek, on the Placerville and Sacramento stage road. Leander or "John" White, driving the forward stage, Mr. Crowder the second, and on reaching the crossing of Deer creek, White found the flood running and the bridge washed away. He hesitated a moment, and meantime the second coach came near. Crowder seeing what was going on advised him not to attempt to cross; this warned the passengers to get out; White, however, thought he could go over easily enough and let his horses plunge into the deep and rapid water. But no sooner had the coach entered the water, then it was swung round and overturned, uncoupling the forward running gear and enabling the horses to escape. The driver, though, fastened by means of the drawn-up leather apron, was floated out, rose two or three times in making efforts to gain the bank, but was taken away by the swift current, and he disappeared under the water.

mining ground; and large quantities of gold have been taken out; there is still some mining going on here now [1880], mostly by Chinamen.

J. S. Meredith opened the first hotel and store at Negro Bar, both being in the same building, in April, 1850. William A. Davidson opened the second store, but was shortly after bought out by A. A. Durfee & Brother. A few months later Rowley & Richardson opened a third store. These were the principal business houses until Folsom was started.

Folsom was laid out by Theodore D. Judah, Richmond Chenery and Samuel O. Bruce, for Captain J. L. Folsom, in 1855. The lots were then sold on the 17th of January, 1856, at public auction, in the City of Sacramento, Col. J. B. Starr, auctioneer. The lots were all sold at this sale. Purchasers commenced building, and the town grew rapidly.

On the 22d day of February following, the Sacramento Valley Railroad was finished to Folsom, and opened. Free excursion trains were run from Sacramento to Folsom. There were about one thousand people present, including Governor Johnson, Judges Murray and Terry, several members of the Senate and Assembly, ex-Governor Foote and many other prominent persons. A cold collation, and champagne *ad libitum*, were supplied gratuitously to the guests.

In the evening a special train was run from Sacramento to Folsom, for the accommodation of people from Sacramento wishing to attend the ball given in Folsom that evening. The train left the Third-street depot at 7:30 P. M., and arrived at Folsom at 9 P. M. The guests were conveyed by omnibuses in waiting to the Meredith Hotel, "under the hill." This building was erected expressly for this occasion, and was thirty feet wide by nearly one hundred feet long, and presented a brilliant appearance, being brightly illuminated.

At 10 P. M. the sound of music announced that the dancing had begun, and in a few moments the floor of the spacious ball-room was alive with flying couples, clad in every variety of costume, male and female, that fancy might suggest and money procure, varying from the rough canvas of the miner or the calico of the shop-girl to the swallowtailed coat of the beau or the low-necked muslin of the city belle.

The supper was superb, and, after partaking thereof, dancing was again in order. At midnight, notice was given that a special train for Sacramento would leave Folsom at one o'clock A. M., but at that hour no passengers appeared, and it was not until five o'clock and broad daylight that the excited dancers be-

Rail operations began February 3, 1856 linking Folsom with Sacramento. By 1861, 1,500 men were employed at the extensive machine shops (car shops) built at the Folsom terminus. In 1856, the first railroad turntable in the west was built in Folsom. In 1869, the operation was transferred to Sacramento.

Soon after my arrival in Sacramento City I felt the powerful lure of the mountains whose dazzling peaks in their white dress, like gentlemen-at-arms, stand watch over the ever pure virgin, New Helvetia. Here one can live freely in beautiful nature with one's own memories. The quite good road led me along the American River, across the dry plain, through the warm oak forest, where the nightingale's sweet song occasionally surprised me and where the California tufted quail returns from the plain to refresh itself in the shade. On past the pleasant taverns, the mile houses, the road gradually rises until it reaches the first mining valleys of the American River. Mormon Island or Natoma, as it was called after a vanished Indian tribe, was the place where I first stayed.

Carl Meyer, 1855

Folsom Historical Society

The railroad was a vital part of Folsom for many years, and boys always did love trains. These two boys are the sons of an engineer.

Dec 27 took the steamer. now so seasick cannot write. stopt at San Francisco one week from there to Sacramento. stopt with Mr White a gentleman from Boston one week. went from there to Mormon Island hired a little Log hut.

january 11 eat Breakfast on my trunk my husband sat down on the floor and I sat myself down on a three legd stool. there we sat and eat our Breakfast. no one can immagine what my feelings were. the first week earnt 23 dollars sewing for the Spanish Ladies the second week earnt 26 dollars.

Unknown Pioneer Woman

gan to realize that dancing is hard work after all, and to wonder why it was they were so tired. We suppose that they found out on the return trip to Sacramento.

Folsom was the terminus of the Sacramento Valley Railroad. A railroad was projected in 1857 to run from Folsom to Marysville. The Company was formed in Marysville, and called the California Central Railroad. They built the bridge across the American River in 1858, and in October, 1861, ran trains into Lincoln. This road was abandoned about 1866.

FLOODS: GREAT DAMAGE AT FOLSOM The *Daily Union* of Monday, January 13th, 1862, has the following:

"Upon Friday night the American river rose sixty feet above low water mark, and destroyed a large amount of property. The old flour mill of Stockton & Coover, built some seven or eight years ago, and the new mill built by them during the last summer in conjunction with Carroll & Moore of this city, were both carried away, and in their course took off the wire suspension bridge of Kinsey & Thompson. The new mill was designed to run nine pair of burrs, and is reported to have cost between $20,000 and $30,000. A large quantity of wheat therein stored, was also lost. The wire bridge was built in the summer of 1856, and cost about $18,000. A wooden bridge, some ten feet lower, had been previously destroyed. The railroad bridge belonging to the California Central Railroad Company, some fifteen feet higher than the wire bridge, and of a single span, is still standing. We are informed that families were taken from the tops of houses in boats, their buildings were carried away, and most of their stock destroyed. A large amount of stock on the lower Stockton road has been lost. Norris' bridge, on the American river, some four miles from its mouth, which withstood the flood of December 9th, gave way on Saturday afternoon, (January 11th), to the still stronger torrent. At about half past four o'clock, two sections of the structure were carried off, and lodged on the north bank of the river, a short distance away. There is now no bridge standing on the American River, that we are aware of, excepting only the railroad bridge at Folsom."

BRIDGES The railroad bridge across the American River was commenced on May 31, 1858. This bridge was on the line of the California Central Railroad, was ninety-two feet above

The suspension bridge (on left) was 50 feet lower than the railroad bridge, and was lost to the floodwaters of 1862. The railroad bridge trestle was damaged and in 1866 was condemned. During the peak of the railroad's operation, trains regularly traveled from Folsom to Roseville and on to Lincoln.

Folsom Historical Society

California Negrobar
October 30 1852

My Dear Selden

... sometimes I am making gruel for the sick now and then cooking oisters sometimes making coffee for the French people strong enough for any man to walk on that has Faith as Peter had. three times a day I set my Table which is about thirty feet in length and do all the little fixings about it such as filling pepper boxes and vinegar cruits and mustard pots and Butter cups. sometimes I am feeding my chickens and then again I am scareing the Hogs out of my kitchen and Driving the mules out of my Dining room.

...your affectionate mother
Mary B Ballou

On the evening of October 20th, 1860, while four miners of the vicinity were seated in the store of Messrs. Pierson & Hackamoller, engaged in a social game of cards, five men with masked faces and pistols in hand entered the store. The first party, supposing that they were a party of miners, bent on a little fun, attempted to set the dog on them, which move was responded by the robbers with a shot, fired at the card players, and the advice if they would remain quiet, they should not be hurt. Upon this proposition being agreed to, they demanded of Mr. Pierson the key to his safe. He told them it was not in the store; whereupon they commenced to beat him with the butt end of their pistols, he warded off the blows and tried to make his escape by a door leading into the family room, which they were determined not to allow him. He was fired upon by one of the villains, the shot entered near the eye, producing almost instant death. Then they took the key from his pocket, and rifled the safe of its contents, and departed. The safe at the time contained a thousand dollars or more. This robbery and murder, unequalled for boldness and daring, produced great excitement, Mr. Pierson being one of the best and most respected citizens.

The Ecklon Bridge (originally known as the Folsom and Ashland Suspension Bridge), which collapsed in 1892 after the suspicious failure of a cable, was the third of several American River crossings that served Folsom residents. Named for its owner, Christian Ecklon, the 30-year-old crossing was a cable suspension toll bridge. The photo shows area residents enjoying this new fishing spot!

the water, with a span of two hundred and sixteen feet; cost, $100,000; and was the only bridge left on the American River by the flood of 1862, caused by the elevation being fifty feet greater than the suspension bridge. The bridge was condemned in 1866, it having sunk in the center and been considered unsafe for some time. It was subsequently sold and taken down some time after 1868.

In 1854 a wooden bridge was built across the American River at Folsom. It was washed away by high water a few years later.

Thompson & Kinsey then obtained a charter for building a bridge across the American River at Folsom in 1861.

This was a wire suspension bridge. The flood of 1862 carried this bridge away on January 10. On March 7, 1862, the work of rebuilding commenced. This is the present structure; it connects Folsom with Ashland, a little town across the river, and is called "The Folsom and Ashland Suspension Bridge;" is of the Halliday Patent; length of span, three hundred and fifty feet between towers; has two cables, eight-hundred feet long, and four towers; weight of bridge, seventy-five tons. Kinsey &

Whitely were the builders. C. L. Ecklon purchased the bridge and franchise in 1871. The tolls are: Foot passenger, both ways, ten cents; team, both ways same day, fifty cents; man on horseback, each way, twelve and one-half cents. The charter runs for twenty-five years from the 3d of February, 1862.

CAR SHOPS. The Sacramento Valley Railroad built its car and machine shops at Folsom in 1861. The buildings consisted of a brick machine shop, sixty feet wide by one hundred and ten feet long; a car shop, also, of brick, forty feet wide by eighty feet long, and a foundry; in all, employing about fifty[1] men. The shops were closed and the machinery moved to Sacramento, December 26, 1869.

During the Washoe excitement, Folsom was the starting point for twenty-one different stage lines running to the northern mines. In April, 1862, it was made the terminus of the overland mail route, which had previously been at Placerville.

BREWERIES. There never have been but two breweries in Folsom. The first was built by Chris Heiler, in 1857, and was run for several years by Raber & Heiler. This was destroyed by fire in 1868.

In 1872, Peter Yager erected a brewery on the foundation of a large store which was destroyed in the destructive fire of 1870. The building, which is made of brick, is a substantial structure, and well adapted for the purpose of a brewery. The di-

From Natoma I proceeded down the lower part of the North Fork. This river is one of the richest in gold in all California. I found the busiest mining life here.

Carl Meyer, 1855

Considering the times, this was a rather tame lot hanging around outside the Buffalo Brewery.

Wednesday evening, January 9th, 1878, Constable J. B. Fisher, of Grizzly Flat, delivered David Branthover to Sheriff Theissen, on a charge of having killed his brother, Adam Branthover, near the above-named place. The facts are as follows: There was some trouble between them in relation to a partnership in a quartz claim. Tuesday, in company of D. T. Loofbourrow, David went to the cabin of the deceased for the purpose of settling the dispute. While comparing accounts, according to Loofbourrow's testimony before A. J. Graham, Justice of the Peace, David frequently gave Adam the lie, and finally, both being much excited, they clinched. During the struggle, a gun in the hand of David went off, the ball striking Adam in the thigh, coming out at the hip; death ensued in less than an hour. Immediately after the affray, David went to the cabin of Fisher and Morey, stated what had occurred, and said that he expected to shoot Adam through the body, but the deceased knocked the gun down; he was not aware at the time that Adam was mortally wounded.

Folsom Historical Society

Saloons did a lively business in Folsom and all over the Gold Country. During the Gold Rush, when coins were not available, the miner would trade a "pinch" of gold dust for a drink.

mensions are, thirty feet front on Sutter street, by one hundred and thirty feet deep, is one story in hight in front, the rear, over the railroad, being three stories high. There is a brewing room adjoining, containing kettle, cooler, & wash-tub. The cellars extend the entire length of the building, being as commodious as any in the county. The daily capacity is about ten barrels, but it has not been taxed that much, the demand not requiring it. The annual sales have been about four hundred and fifty barrels.

FLOURING MILL. Caners' Flouring Mill was built in 1866, on the corner of Wool street and the Railroad; the mill was operated about two years, when it was closed. The building, a three-story brick, was purchased by B. N. Bugbey, and used by him as a wine cellar, the third floor being rented as a hall to the societies of Folsom. The building was burned about the year 1871.

Natoma Mills were built by Edward Stockton in June, 1866, using the three-story brick building formerly occupied by the Wheeler House; the power was taken from the Natoma ditch, and using two runs of stone; discontinued.

There are in Folsom at present [1880] two hotels, two livery stables, four grocery stores, three hardware and tin stores, two drug stores, one dry goods store, one variety store, two lumber yards, one bank, one furniture store, one wagon and blacksmith shop, four blacksmith shops, one harness shop, one express office, one bakery, two restaurants, two barber shops, two butcher shops, one brewery, two shoe shops, one gun store, two jewelers (repairing), one fruit drying establishment, one distillery and winery, ten saloons.

THE FOLSOM TELEGRAPH. The *Folsom Telegraph* is the only paper published in Folsom. It was started, in 1860, under the name of *Folsom Weekly Telegraph.* On January 1, 1861, the paper was changed to a semi-weekly, as the *Folsom Semi-Weekly Telegraph,* C Killmer and W. M. Penry, publishers and editors; July 16, 1861, C. Killmer and O. D. Avaline, publishers and editors; and December 3, 1861, O. D. Avaline became sole proprietor. Avaline died, December 26, 1863; Mrs. Avaline continued the paper, with P. J. Hopper as editor. On January 2, 1864, the paper was changed to a weekly, under its present name, *Folsom Telegraph.*

FIRES. Folsom has suffered heavily from fires, at different times. May 8, 1866, a fire burned "Whiskey Row," and a number of buildings on Sutter and Decatur streets, including the office of the *Folsom Telegraph.* August 31, 1866, the Hotel de France and a number of contiguous buildings were burned.

The Folsom Theater was destroyed by fire, June 27, 1871. In 1871, a fire destroyed all of Chinatown, Patterson's Hotel,

As far as the eye can see all has suddenly come to life. The overseer's reverberating gong or trumpet starts off to their day's work groups of various nationalities, among which the Chinese are the most striking. Crowbars resound on the hard stone, gold scales rattle in the gravel and the blustering quartz mill can be heard above all while the whistle of the steam-engine screams through the animated valley.

Carl Meyer, 1855

Many vineyards were planted in the area in the 1850s and 1860s. It was California's first "wine country." These people were culling grapes from their recent harvest.

Folsom Historical Society

Building a dredge on Poverty Bar on the American River, 1870s.

Jim, and Jim Patterson, Indians, indicted for the murder of Charles Gay, on June 26th, 1861, near Salmon Falls, found guilty of murder in the first degree, and sentenced to suffer the extreme penalty of the law. Their execution took place on November 1st, in the jail yard. Their bodies were permitted to hang twenty minutes, when they were cut down, placed in coffins and delivered to some Indians, who conveyed them to Gold Hill to Captain John, Chief of the tribe, who burnt them in due form.

and part of Addison's lumber yard. May 6, 1872, a fire broke out in Smith, Campbell & Jolly's store, and destroyed all the buildings in the block, with the exception of the office of the *Folsom Telegraph.* Among these buildings were Meredith's drug store and Farmer's blacksmith shop. The loss was about one hundred and thirty thousand dollars.

COBBLE STONES. For a number of years the trade in cobble stones, which were gathered along the American River, was very large. This district supplied the great bulk of the paving stones for San Francisco. Prior to the completion of the Sacramento Valley Railroad, the stones were loaded into scows and taken to Sacramento, and there transferred to schooners for the Bay. In 1856, a man named White engaged largely in the shipment of paving stones.

In 1863, the cobble pits at Texas Hill became the property of the Sacramento Valley Railroad Company. Millions of tons of cobbles have been shipped - much the greater part of which has gone to San Francisco.

NEGRO HILL. The first mining work done in the vicinity of Negro Hill was on the east side, adjoining the river, by a company of Mormons, in the year 1848, soon after, but in the same year, a company of Spaniards went to work on the south side of the hill, in Spanish Ravine, from a strip of ground about a thousand feet in length by one and a-half feet in width, and three feet in depth they took out over seven thousand dollars. The next work was in a deep sand bank just at the mouth of Spanish Ravine, in the fall of 1849, by August B. Newhall, from Lynn, Mass., a Negro by the name of Kelsey, a Methodist preacher, and other Negroes; this locality was called Little Negro Hill, it being located between the river and the present Negro Hill. The gravel in said sand bank paid three hundred dollars and upwards, per day, to a company of five men.

The same year (1852) Dewitt Stanford, a brother of Leland Stanford, built a grocery store at Negro Hill, as did Horace and Frank Barton. Another store was built about the same time by Ben. Avery, our late minister to China, he opened with a lot of drugs, Yankee notions, etc. A short time later, about the fall of 1852 or spring of 1853, the Chinese began to flock in the camp, and built on another portion of the flat. So that by the end of 1853, the town could boast of a thousand or twelve hundred inhabitants, with stores of every description, saloons and dance houses by the dozen, and all seemed to do a thriving business.

We have to refer to a visit of Judge Lynch at this place in the time when Thomas Jenkins and Richard Rickard were building their store in 1852; a Negro claiming the illustrious name of Andrew Jackson, stole a specimen worth about $10.00, and some clothing from the residence of Mr. Keith, the blacksmith, for which he was hung to a tree, near the Negro quarters, by a mob, before noon.

Folsom's Cohn General Store, pictured here in 1890.

Folsom Historical Society

Spanish Camp, (near Folsom) January 12th, 1863 On Saturday last, the 10th of January, this camp was visited by a band of guerrillas, who had as little respect for the rights of property and law as there is possible in man. About 7 o'clock four men—W. Porter, C. S. Smith, P. West and Ike Hitchcock, seated themselves in the store of W. E. Riebsam for a game of whist, Messrs. Adams and Riebsam were standing near. Suddenly four men entered, each armed with a large navy revolver, cocked and held at the party around the whist table. They ordered all in the store to remain quiet, which order it was useless to resist; one of the robbers put up his revolver, turned around to coil rope, cut off several lengths and tied the men in the store. They then searched each man, taking every valuable and attempted to open the safe, the key of which they had taken from Mr. Riebsam, but failing, they forced Mr. R. to unlock it for them. They soon rifled the safe of its contents, but there being but little cash in it they were greatly exasperated and departed.

Gambling and drinking were favorite past times.

California Negrobar
October 30 1852

My Dear Selden

... I suppose you would like to know what I'm doing in this gold region. well I will try to tell you what my work is here in this muddy Place. All the kitchen that I have is four posts stuck down into the ground and covered over the top with factory cloth no floor but the ground. this is a Boarding House kitchen. there is a floor in the dining room and my sleeping room covered with nothing but cloth. we are at work in a Boarding House...

...your affectionate mother
Mary B Ballou

In 1855 a lot of drunken white fellows on Negro Hill attacked the Negro quarters and in the fight one Negro was killed, for which Mr. Drew and others were arrested and tried at Coloma but were acquitted.

Growler's Flat was opened in 1852, by Henry Down, an English sailor, who was always growling, hence the name.

Massachusetts Flat was opened in 1854, by Dr. Townsend. All paid well. At Jenny Lind Flat one night in 1853, a young man borrowed blankets to sleep in, the next morning he had forgotten about this fact, and walked off with the blankets; a crowd went after him and brought him back, flogged him until the blood trickled down his heels; they then took up a subscription in money and gave it to him with the advice never to steal again.

SALMON FALLS. Located on the banks of the South Fork of the American river, at the mouth of Sweetwater creek. The name of the town was derived from the cataract in the American river near the site of the town, whither the Indians used to come down from the mountains to catch salmon, of which the river abounded. Early in 1849 very rich diggings had been discovered by Mormons at Higgins' Point, about a quarter of a mile below town, close to the river, and called after Higgins.

The first bridge across the American river here was built in 1853, this was washed away and another one was put up; the bridge property being a very well paying business, this being the main road from Sacramento to all those mining camps in the northern part of this county to all the river bars on the Middle and North Forks of the American river, and to all the mines beyond there in Placer county. In 1856, Mr. Raun sold out his interest in all those bridges to Richards and Pearish, and later Mr. Richards was the sole owner of this bridge. The railroad, however, which took away the travel from this road and the giving out of the river bars, did not give a profitable outlook, and since the high-water washed away the bridge for the second time it has not been rebuilt.

The town that in a short time did grow from a few Mormon huts to a community of some note, with a population of about 3,000, with many stores, and other pertainings of a mining town, that could make some show with three well built up streets, with good paying mines.

PRAIRIE CITY. This place is located two miles south of Folsom, in Granite township, on the hills on or near Alder Creek. Mining commenced here in 1853, on the completion of the Natoma Water and Mining Company's ditch to this point. The water reached Rhodes' Diggings, about one mile farther

This dramatic rail accident occurred outside Folsom in 1889. Rail accidents were frequent before the turn of the century. Between 3 and 25 rail accidents occurred per day in the US. More than 10,000 people per year lost their lives in rail accidents.

Courtesy of the California History Room, California State Library, Sacramento, CA

California Negrobar
October 30 1852

My Dear Selden

I will tell you a little of my bad feelings. on the 9 of September there was a little fight took place in the store. I saw them strike each other through the window in the store. one went and got a pistol and started towards the other man. I never go into the store but your mothers tender heart could not stand that so I ran into the store and Beged and plead with him not to kill him for eight or ten minutes not to take his Life for the sake of his wife and three little children to spare his life and then I ran through the Dining room into my sleeping room and Buried my Face in my bed so as not to hear the sound of the pistol and wept Biterly.

. ..your affectionate
mother
Mary B Ballou

Folsom Historical Society

Folsom was the hub for all types of services, first for the miners and later for the farmers, ranchers and other residents. There were several blacksmiths in the area until the 1920s.

The town of Salmon Falls here will have a wonderful future. Two bridges, very well built and in good taste, already span the river, and a good road leads to the abandoned mining town, Pilot Hill, in the northern part of the Eldorado region.

Carl Meyer, 1855

up the creek, early in June, 1853. The miners came flocking in from all directions, and Prairie City began to assume the importance of a city, in fact, as well as in name. This was the business town for several mining camps, Rhodes Diggings, Willow Springs, Bill Diggings, Alder Creek. Rhodes' Diggings laid some pretentions to having a town of its own; John H. Gass and Colonel Z. Hagan built a steam quartz mill in 1855, and a French company built a large quartz mill in 1857, costing fifty thousand dollars; this mill paid wonderfully well for a time.

TEXAS HILL was a mining camp just below Negro Bar, on the American River, and extensive operations were carried on there until 1855.

BEAMS BAR was named after Jerry Beam. It is situated one half mile below Alabama Bar, on the south side of the American River. The Bar was first worked in the summer of 1849 by what was called Beam's Company, which consisted of twelve men. The Bar, as mined by Beam's Company, did not include any part of the river bed, which was under water in summer time. This Bar was wonderfully rich until worked out. The men of Beam's Company considered they had had a poor day if the result was less than a pound of gold per man.

In the early summer of 1852, a fight occurred for the possession of this claim, caused by an attempt to jump the claim by a party of fourteen men, headed by a man named Schofield. This party claimed a right to the ground under previous location, but, from the final settlement, it is doubtful if they ever had such a right. The men of the Beam's Bar Company were waiting in their camp, on the bank of the river, for the water to go down. They had noticed that there was a large camp of men about one-quarter of a mile from them, but thought nothing of it, till one morning, about daybreak, while they were getting their breakfast, the Schofield party appeared in full force with their shovels, wheelbarrows and other mining implements, and descended the bank to the claim, and took possession thereof. One of Beam's Bar Company by the name of Johnson went down, and informed them that the claim belonged to them, the Beam's Bar Company, and that, so far from having vacated it, they were only waiting for the water to subside sufficiently to allow effective work. Schofield inquired, "Is that all?" On being answered "yes," he turned to his party and said, "Go to work, boys."

About this time the Beam's Bar Company jumped in and began work also. A lively skirmish ensued, in which spades, shovels and knives were freely used, not a shot being fired. The Schofield party retired badly demoralized, a brother of the head of the party having been nearly scalped by a blow from the edge of a spade, which finally resulted in his death, some eighteen months later.

Although some miners built shacks or small wooden houses, many had only a tent for shelter.

"I remember when the superintendent rushed out where I was standing by my horse, ready for the start. He was white with excitement. 'Ride as fast as you can, young man' he said as he locked the pouch, 'because President Lincoln's inaugural message is in here."

William Cates
Pony Express Rider

...who carried the inaugural address between Fort Kearny, Nebraska Territory & Folsom, California

California State Archives

Second only in notoriety to the cruel and blood-thirsty Joaquin Murietta was the celebrated Tom Bell, the "Gentleman Highwayman."

He was convicted of grand larceny in 1855, and sentenced to five years in the State Prison, at Angel Island.

In May, 1855, he made his escape with half a dozen other prisoners.

He soon gathered about him a band of choice spirits, whom, by his superior education and ability, he was able to control. He is said to have worn a suit of armor under his clothes for protection, but this is probably untrue. There were in a band about fifty men, those in the extreme north being [under the] leadership of Montague Lyan, alias Monte Jack, a blood-thirsty villain of repulsive appearance. Their retreat was in the recesses of the mountains, from which they issued in small bands to commit their depredations. During the spring and summer of 1856, scarcely a night passed but some lonely traveler was permitted to stare into the muzzle of a persuading revolver, while he was being relieved of his property.

As far back as 1851, the Natoma Company played a role in Folsom history providing granite quarrying, agriculture, vineyards and hydro-electric power. After the turn of the century Natoma Company began gold dredging operations and an estimated $100 million in gold was taken from the area.

THE NATOMA WATER AND MINING COMPANY. This Company, at present the largest owner of water rights in the county, was organized in 1851. A. P. Catlin, now living at Sacramento, was the originator of the enterprise. Associated with him were Judge Thomas, H. Williams, Craig and Berry, William Jarvis, now at Folsom, John Bennett and Henry Robinson, then and now living at San Francisco. The main canal was commenced in 1851, taking its water from a point on the south Fork of the American River, two miles above Salmon Falls. The length of the main canal is about twenty miles; the length of the branches for irrigation, etc., we have not been able to learn.

The cost of the canal, branches and reservoirs to date amounts to about one hundred and seventy-five thousand dollars. The canal, from its commencement, runs through a mining country that, without the water furnished by this ditch, would be comparatively valueless. The canal runs through Natoma Township, which it reached in 1852; in 1853 the ditch was finished to Prairie City, and reached Folsom in 1854.

1. Two sources report vastly different figures.

Dry Diggings, Placerville, 1851. Note the Round Tent store at the back left. It can still be seen in 1865 images as well. Most likely it was rebuilt as many of the early structures were lost to fire.

Chapter 7: Placerville (Hangtown, Ravine City)

Placerville was incorporated in virtue of an act that for the proof of having passed State Senate as well as Assembly bears the signatures of Charles S. Fairfax, Speaker of Assembly; Samuel Purdy, President of Senate, approved May 13, 1854, John Bigler Governor.

Thus Placerville became a city, after having passed through nearly six years of most eventful experience, from the date of its first settlement; some of these having been the reason to impose upon the young town the name of

HANGTOWN, under which it was going for several years, known by all miners of California up to this day, and not seldom used even now after about thirty years. We have got before

There is a good deal of sin & wickedness going on here, Stealing, lying, Swearing, Drinking, Gambling & murdering. There is a great deal of gambling carried on here. Almost every public House is a place for Gambling, & this appears to be the greatest evil that prevails here. Men make & lose thousands in a night...

S. SHUFELT, 1850
Written from
Placerville

A man by the name of F. L. Smith was murdered on April 23d, 1862, on the Ogilsby road, about 21 miles east of Placerville. A rifle ball broke his spine, passing through his heart. Two young men traveling the same road on foot, heard the report of a gun, hurried to the spot, and arriving where the murdered man fell, saw a man picking up his hat and a rifle. Some dispute arose between the parties, but the two being unarmed left after the murderer threatened to shoot them also. They went to the Goodwin Mountain House, to give the alarm, and on returning to the spot and searching, they discovered the murdered man, who had been dragged about 100 yards below the road into the chapparel. A rope was tied around his body. The body was brought to Placerville for burial. The murderer was arrested by Deputy Sheriff Chapman, two days after, near Ringgold, and lodged in jail. The name of the prisoner was C. W. Smith, his case was tried in the District Court before Judge Myers, and as the evidence was entirely circumstantial, but so conclusive as to leave not the shadow of doubt of his guilt, he was convicted of murder in the first degree and on November 24th, 1862, sentenced to be hung on January 9th, 1863.

Main Street Placerville, late 1800s

Steve Crandell Collection, Restoration by Steve Crandell

us three different statements of the affair that caused the above name, as given by three most distinguished citizens and oldest pioneers, and we think it is the best to make space here for all three of them, on account of some varieties in the different statements that are corroborant and supplement one to another.

"Allow me to give you the true version," says Judge Grimshaw of Daylor's ranch, Sacramento County: "In the Summer of 1848, three ranchers residing in what is now Sacramento County, William Daylor, Jared Sheldon and Perry McCoon, with a number of Indians in their employ, were mining in Weber creek at a point of about one hundred yards below the crossing of the road leading from Diamond Springs to Placerville. One morning the vaquero, who had charge of the cavalada (tame horses) informed his employers that he had discovered some new dry diggings; exhibiting at the same time some specimens of gold which he had picked up. One of the white men went to the place, indicated by the Indian, but found that the diggings were not sufficiently better than those on the creek to justify them in moving their camp. When prospectors came along they were referred to the new location, which up to January, 1849, went by the name of the "Old Dry Diggings."

"One night during that month, three men were in a saloon, tent or hut at the Old Dry Diggings, engaged in a game of poker. In due time one of the party got 'broke.' The proprietor of the place was fast asleep. The one who had lost his money suggested to his companions that he had gold dust on hand, and proposed that he should be robbed. The proprietor was awoke, a pistol presented to his head, and told to disclose the whereabouts of his hidden treasure. This he did, the robbers divided the spoil, threatened the saloon keeper with certain death if he disclosed anything about the matter, and resumed their game.

"The next day the saloon keeper mustered courage to tell some of his friends about the robbery, the affair became noised about; the three men were arrested, tried by the miners and sentenced to be flogged, and the judgment executed with the promptness which characterized that kind of criminal procedure. The criminals were then ordered to leave. In a few days two of the men, under the influence of whiskey went about the camp, intimating that the men who were engaged in the trial were 'spotted', that they would not live to flog another man, etc.

"A meeting was called, the two men were arrested and hung on the leaning oak tree in the hay yard below Elstner's ElDorado Saloon, the same tree on which afterwards other malefactors expiated their crimes.

"For many years the camp went by the name of Hangtown, to distinguish it from other dry diggings. Daylor, Sheldon and McCoon remained on the creek until the fall of 1848, when they returned to their homes on the Sheldon and Daylor grant in Sacramento County.

"Capt. Charles M. Weber, of Weber's embarcadero (or Tuleburg) later Stockton, established a camp and trading post

Central House, T. C. Fisk, Proprietor, Placerville, 1888

The accumulation of disorderly, unruly and desperate fellows and the crimes they had committed, had caused the people of El Dorado county at various instances to take the law in their own hands, but as the population was rapidly growing, it became time to have the execution of the lawful sentences by the officers of the law. James Logan, for the murder of Fennel at Coon Hollow, and Wm. Lipsey, for killing Powelson at Cold Springs, were the first to be convicted of murder in the District Court of El Dorado county. Their execution took place, according to the sentence of Judge Howell, on Friday, November 3d, 1854. The assemblage of people to see the unusual sight was the largest ever known in El Dorado county. From early morning of that day every thoroughfare leading to Coloma from all parts of the county, far as well as near, were thronged with one continuous line or mass of people on foot, on horseback, in wagons, carts. This procession a sample-carte of nationalities and races, all seemed under the same influence, as though an invisible power directed their steps towards Coloma; a dense mass of human beings, while the hillsides were covered with thousands more.

The crowd was estimated at from six to eight thousand persons. The execution took place at Coloma, on the hill where the cemetery now [1883] is located.

Mr. & Mrs. M. O'Keefe. O'Keefe's Furniture and Undertaking Business, Main Street, Placerville California, 1880s.

The rain has rendered the road nearly impassable across the plain, and in coming to a swampy-looking spot, I reined up my horse for a minute, to consider the case. I gently urged the animal on—the poor creature obeyed, put his nose nearly to the ground, and his feet tenderly forward; we entered the water, knee-deep, one step more, down went the horse to the girths, rolled over on one side, and lodged me in the mud and water we were floundering hopelessly in the slough. I had just got myself clear of the horse, but to get the horse as clear of the mud was the matter. A good tempered American just then came up, and while I was endeavouring to relieve the animal, he said, "Wall, stranger, I guess you're kinder mired down." I agreed in his opinion, when he dismounted, waded knee-deep into the mud-hole, and combining our strength, we got the horse out. This kindheartedness I never knew to leave the true native American miner of California; they are benevolent and generous, sudden in action, and excitable as they may be in temper.

Sir Henry Vere Huntley, 1856

on the same locality and gave the creek the name which it has borne to the present day."

Mr. E. N. Strout, for long years a citizen of El Dorado county, says: "In 1848, and the early part of 1849, Placerville and surroundings were known as 'Old Dry Diggings.' At that time there were organized bands of desperadoes, with signs, passwords and grips, and with chiefs and lieutenants, who lay in wait in and around the mining camps, ready for plunder and murder, either for gain or revenge. Murders and robberies were frequent along the branches of the South and Middle Forks of the American river, and finally found their way to the mining camp on the north branch of Weber creek—Old Dry Diggings, now Placerville. A Frenchman who kept a trading post in Log Cabin ravine—now Bedford avenue—was known to have considerable gold dust, and he was selected by the 'Owls'—the name of the organization—as their victim to be robbed. Four of this band, composed of one American, one Mexican and two Frenchmen, made a descent on the post and robbed the merchant of his gold dust and such other valuables as they wanted, while the owner was powerless to resist; but the robbers were marked men from that moment. The Frenchman gave the alarm and the vigilantes started in pursuit of the robbers, who were captured, brought to trial, condemned and executed, except one of the Frenchmen, who escaped after sentence had been pronounced. The execution took place under a white oak tree of gigantic size that stood on the south bank of Hangtown creek, now the northwest corner of Main and Coloma streets, on February 12th, 1849. George G. Blanchard's brick building covers the stump of the tree. W. T. Sayward, Esq., of San Francisco, who was Deputy Prefect for the Old Dry Diggings at the time, declared that murder was clearly proven against the culprits, as well as robbery. Their bodies were buried on the north side of the creek. The *Mountain Democrat's* office was subsequently erected over their graves, and said paper published there for more than twenty years."

THE RAVINE CITY, as Placerville was called also. Even the most sanguine of the inhabitants of this place, in the spring of 1850, scarcely dared to hope that their village would ever attain a greater dignity than that of a temporary mining camp. All those that had mined here during 1849 asserted that the mines were worked out in this vicinity, and a sort of general stampede followed, so that the town during the early part of the summer of 1850, was well nigh deserted.

Placerville saw another season of prosperity when the mines in Washoe district began to attract the attention of the mining world, and the flushest and liveliest time commenced in her streets. There were no vacant houses, hotels were plenty and all were full, stores were constantly receiving additions to their stock, the pioneer stages were running daily and always crowded with passengers coming and going to Washoe; Baker's fast freight was doing a large business besides, money was plenty and everybody prospering and consequently contented and happy, but the discouragement produced by causes beyond the control of men, did not fail to follow: No sooner was the Central Pacific

The son of a Southern planter in 1850 came to Placerville with an old slave, as a sort of a bodyguard, to view the situation. One night the old darkey dreamed that there was a rich deposit of nuggets beneath the cabin of a neighbor and he seriously told his master of his dream. The young Southerner laughed it off. A few nights afterward, the old darkey had the same dream again. He became so impressed with it that he insisted on his young master giving it attention and acting upon it. The easy going young Southerner bought the ground, more to satisfy the whim of his bodyguard than any other reason, and then set him to work developing his dream. The first day of work yielded $20,000 and that was probably about one-half of what they took out of the ground he purchased as dreamland.

Charles Peters, 1849

Ohio House Bar, Placerville, California, 1880s.

At Perkin, in the lower part of Mud Springs township, three Chilenos became engaged in a fight on Sunday, March 18th, 1866, the result of which was the killing of Casas Rojas and Marcellius Bellasque by Pedro Pablo. The murderer was arrested by other Chilenos present and handed over to special constable Bailey, who started to Shingle Springs. The night being dark and stormy, and under cover of the darkness the prisoner freed himself from the handcuffs, jumped from the horse and escaped. The sheriff was notified, and sent Under-Sheriff Hume and Jailor Cartheche in pursuit of the murderer, who finally was discovered by a brother of one of the murdered men in a quartz mill near Diamond Springs, on the following Wednesday. He informed Constables Bailey and Shrewsberry of his whereabouts, and they arrested and brought the culprit to Placerville; where he was examined before Justice Sherwood and committed to jail awaiting the action of the Grand Jury.

Formerly Mud Springs, the township of El Dorado, 1856.

Steve Crandell Collection, Restoration by Steve Crandell

Railroad finished as far as Cisco, and the cars were running up to the latter place, a distance of about ninety miles from Sacramento City, and the Pioneer Stage Co., as well as Baker's fast freight were moving their whole stock of coaches, fast freight wagons, teams etc., over to the Dutch Flat route carrying with them scores of men in their employ and dependent on them for their support. This was the most striking and sudden change for the whole country; but more so for Placerville particularly, and business began to slow then decline rapidly; but the depression came to a standstill, people began to throw off their discouragement, and appreciate the resources that this city possesses for the present subsistence, with a good prospect for future wealth in the lumber business, having an unlimited quality of the finest timber within 15 to 18 miles; and by means of agricultural and mining work, with a large extent of splendid agricultural land all around and a good many of the richest mines close by.

Placerville is the principal commercial place in the county, and is harboring the County Court seat of El Dorado since twenty-six years now, and the County Hospital two years more. The daily mail from Sacramento commenced to arrive here about the middle of August, 1854, and the citizens ever since have enjoyed this comfort. The importance of Placerville may be seen also out of the number of stage lines that were running from this place to all parts of this county, to Sacramento, to the Southern mines and over the Sierra Nevada to Washoe. On account of their railroad, however, the Placervilleians had no good luck. For the purpose of taking the matter under consideration, a railroad-meeting was held here as early as November 16, 1854; the proposition was to build an extension to the Sacramento Valley Railroad, then only planned, but ready to be commenced, from the terminus at Folsom up to Placerville, but the subject rested after some agitation without further proceedings. The agitation was renewed in 1863, and a public meeting held in Upper Placerville, on February, 16th, but the result was the same.

The communication of Placerville with other parts of the county or with the county further on by means of county or toll-roads is quite a perfect one; eight or ten good mountain roads run from this place.

The first overland mail stage arrived in Placerville on Monday, July 19, 1858, at 10 o'clock P. M., and many who were aware of the event hailed it with ardent manifestations of joy. Mr. W. M. Cary illuminated his new hotel; from the lateness of the hour however, many had retired and from their ignorance of the arrival had not the satisfaction of expressing their joy upon the occasion. In order that all might have an opportunity of expressing their sentiments, large posters were distributed through the city next day, announcing that a grand jubilee would be held on the plaza that evening.

Wells Fargo Stage Line, late 1860s.

Mead Simpson Collection, Restoration by Steve Crandell

Two miners in 1859 were travelling the trail from White Rock to Placerville when they came to a ravine two miles from the town. There three men were picking and shovelling dirt into a line of sluice boxes while a foppish-looking individual stood upon the bank directing operations. He was dressed in what then was fashionable attire. A part of this was a ruffled bosom white shirt, a yellow vest; a black silk cravat wound twice around a stiff white collar and on his head a tall plug hat. The two miners on ascertaining he was the owner of the claim; was too proud to work it himself and employed the three men to do it for him, were at first disgusted and then became angry as they discussed the situation. According to their logic a man who would not work in a placer claim himself, should not own one. After considerable argument, threats and dicker, they bought the claim and ordered the foppish owner to clear out. They then made a gift of the claim to the three men who were working in it. These men were from Georgia and in six weeks' time cleaned up enough to start back to their Georgia homes with over $6000 apiece.

Charles Peters, 1849

Main Street Placerville First Gas Light, 1858. Round Tent Store on Left.

Ah Soo, a Chinaman, on the 19th of September, 1859, stabbed one of his countrymen, Ching Sam, with a bowie-knife at Placerville, inflicting a wound upon him of which he died a few days later. He was arrested and arraigned for trial in the District Court, where the evidence clearly showed that the deed had been committed in cold blood and without the shadow of provocation. The jury returned a verdict of guilty of murder in the first degree. But before the sentence could be pronounced upon him, the unfortunate wretch hanged himself, thus saving the county the expense by cheating the gallows.

The great banking houses of San Francisco, doing the express business all over the State, had their offices at Placerville from the earliest time, and other express firms branched off from their offices to bring the express comfort to other places higher up in the mountains. The Alta Telegraph Company commenced work to connect Sacramento with most all the mining places of Northern mines, taking a wire from said place through El Dorado, Placer, Nevada counties up to Sierra county; but the connection from Sacramento to Placerville, Coloma and Auburn was not finished before spring of 1854. The first newspaper in the county was started at Placerville, and this city has supported two good weekly newspapers all the time since; for a long while there were even three papers kept up and seemed to make it a profitable investment.

INDUSTRY. The first foundry was built and set up in the fall of 1855; the first casting was done there on February 18, 1856. A circular sawmill was put up in the spring of 1853. Brick had been manufactured at Placerville in quantities to sell, since spring of 1852.

The northern and southwestern part of El Dorado county abounds in what is generally known as soap weed or soap root. Some ingenious fellow, got an idea that this root, could be used instead of horse hair in the upholstering business; a trial was made and the result of it is, that two Placerville firms have about a hundred Chinamen engaged in the fall of the year gathering the soap root. Tons of it are being bailed and shipped to Sacramento, and used for upholstering of matresses, etc., under the name of "Excelsior hair."

The introduction of gas light with which the city of Placerville was supplied in the fall of 1858, could be called a great achievement of her citizens. Of other industries there are two breweries here. A large fruit drying establishment has been started of later years in Upper Placerville. A soap factory was started in 1861.

FIRES AT PLACERVILLE. Up to the year of 1856, from the time of the first settlement, Placerville, contrary to most other mining places, had been spared from the fiend; but on April 15, 1856, while a great part of the population were assembled in the Placerville theater, to greet McKean Buchanan in the character of "Richelieu," a fire broke out in the Iowa House on Sacramento street, spread with rapidity over the neighboring buildings.

An incident of bravery occurred in connection with this fire, that deserves to be mentioned in history. After the inmates of the Iowa House had rushed out of this building in utmost confusion and haste, and just when the firemen repaired to the burning building, they were appalled at hearing Mrs. Rockwell, in the extreme agony, crying that her youngest child had been left, lying asleep in one of the rooms of the burning building. The danger was imminent; but Master Jackson L. Ober, a son of Dr. Ober, and an attache of the Neptunes, a youth of 14

But many, very many, that come here meet with bad success & thousands will leave their bones here. Others will lose their health, contract diseases that they will carry to their graves with them. Some will have to beg their way home, & probably one half that come here will never make enough to carry them back. But this does not alter the fact about the gold being plenty here, but shows what a poor frail being man is, how liable to disappointments, disease & death.

S. SHUFELT, 1850
Written from
Placerville

Zeisz Building, California Brewery, and Cool and Placerville Stage Lines Placerville, California.

A man by the name of Jesse Hendricks, an employee of the South Fork canal company, mysteriously disappeared from his section on the canal, some eight miles above Placerville, about May 25, 1870, and notwithstanding the most careful search by a large number of men, no traces could be found; and the general supposition ran that the man had been murdered by Indians, and suspicion rested upon White Rock Jack, the notorious Indian desperado. On December 19, 1876, a deer hunter discovered on the South Fork of the American river, about seven miles above Placerville, two sections of a human skull, one of which he found near the bank of the river, the other about 50 feet higher up, on top of a bluff. Coroner Collins, after being informed of these facts, went up with a party to investigate the locality, on December 21st. They went to the big flume on the old Jack Johnson ranch, and thence directly down to the river; near the river they found the two pieces of skull and a miner's shovel. Further up they discovered a boot containing the bones of a human foot, and still further up another boot containing the bones of a foot and the leg from the knee down.

The Druids in front of the Cary House in 1899. The Cary House still graces Main Street in Placerville and is still open for business.

years, took the fearful risk, and boldly pushed his way through the flame and smoke to the room where the child lay sleeping, unconscious of its danger. He took up the child in his arms and cautiously wending his way back, escaped, and placed it in its mother's arms uninjured; just as the burning building fell in.

The year 1871 saw the springing up—or rather the "rolling up"—of the rink mania, and most every town was anxious to have its own skating-rink. Placerville, of course, took the lead in El Dorado county, and Mud Springs, Shingle Springs, Georgetown, Coloma and others followed to procure or build up a hall for this purpose. Messrs. Creighton & Childs built a new two-story building for this enterprise, now Sierra Hall, which was opened September 1st, 1871, and as long as the people took a fancy to this healthy exercise the hall was crowded every night, and old and young, gentlemen and ladies, all were amusing themselves on the rolling skates, and for quite a while all other public places were deserted, the skating rink absorbing all interest for amusement and entertainment.

Teamsters round the bend below Cave Rock at Lake Tahoe, Nevada 1860s.

Chapter 8: Lake Tahoe & The High Sierras

The scenery of the thus enclosed part of the State of California is classified among the most magnificent in the world; everywhere there is something worth seeing, whether it be the quietly pastoral or grandly picturesque. Fountain and lake, forest and meadow, peak and valley make up this section of the western slope of the Sierra Nevada. On this range are found such prominent and noble points as Park Peak, Mount Tallac, Crystal Peak, Thompson's Peak and Pyramid Peak; besides innumerable lakelets of beauty, such as Fallen Leaf Lake, Look Lake, Silver Lake, Clear Lake, Lake Tallac and valley Lake.

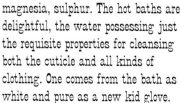

All along the northern shore there are springs of boiling hot water coming to the surface, containing lime, magnesia, sulphur. The hot baths are delightful, the water possessing just the requisite properties for cleansing both the cuticle and all kinds of clothing. One comes from the bath as white and pure as a new kid glove.

Caroline M. Churchill, 1881

Tallac Mountain, Fallen Leaf Lake, 1860s.

We tramped a long time on level ground, and then toiled laboriously up a mountain about a thousand miles high and looked over. No lake there. We descended on the other side, crossed the valley and toiled up another mountain three or four thousand miles high, apparently, and looked over again. No lake yet. We sat down tired and perspiring, and hired a couple of Chinamen to curse those people who had beguiled us. Thus refreshed, we presently resumed the march with renewed vigor and determination. We plodded on, two or three hours longer, and at last the Lake burst upon us—a noble sheet of blue water lifted six thousand three hundred feet above the level of the sea, and walled in by a rim of snow-clad mountain peaks that towered aloft full three thousand feet higher still!

Mark Twain, 1872

El Dorado lays claim to a portion of that unequalled sheet of water, Lake Bigler, the principal inlet of the lake—Emerald Bay—being in the county [El Dorado, California].

It is located on the eastern side of the central ridge of the Sierra Nevada. According to the observations of the United States geographical surveying corps, under command of Lieut. George M. Wheeler, the altitude of the lake is 6,202 feet above the level of the sea; that of Tahoe City, 6,251, and of Hot Springs, 6,237 feet. The water of the lake being shed from the solid granite and volcanic mountains that compose its boundaries by more than thirty streams, is extremely pure and clear, and when in a state of quietness, one can observe fish and other objects most distinct and perfect to the depth of from thirty to forty feet; it is of blue color and very cold, but never freezes in the winter. The temperature 800 feet below the surface always remains at 39.2°, the point of maximum density of fresh pure water; at the surface in the hottest weather, the temperature rises to 68°, and in the coldest sinks to 38° only. The deepest soundings ever made were 2,800 feet. The greatest length of the lake is 21.6 miles; the greatest breadth 12 miles; and the area of the whole sheet of water is about 195 square miles; El Dorado county is entitled to claim nearly one-third of this area as located within her lines. The water is as buoyant as any other pure water, and it is as safe for sailing crafts as any. No more danger than what is common to other places need be feared, either from wind or waves; though no Indian would dare to cross the lake, affirming their belief that an evil spirit would draw them to the bottom, if they would make an attempt.

The bed of Lake Tahoe, by some is supposed to be the crater of an extinct volcano, and to be unfathomable. There are some indications of undoubtable volcanic origin: the masses of scorious or calcereous rock, mentioned already in Fremont's narrative, scattered all about the lake shore and along the banks of the Truckee river; a small conical mound, evidently created by solfataras, may be seen near by, a little to the northwest of Tahoe City; and the occasional occurrence of hot springs on the lake shore as well as in the lake, are evidence enough for this theory. Proof of the later assertion is an incident that was witnessed in September, 1866, from Saxton's saw-mill, by a

Webster's Station, Sugar Loaf Mountain, Webster's Station appears on the 1861 mail contract as a Pony Express station. The station, which stood on the Placerville Carson Road, began as an original C.O.C. & P.P. Express Co. station in April 1860. It also served as a stop for teamsters and the stage lines until the late 1860s. Travelers also knew Webster's as Sugar Loaf House named for a nearby rocky mountain. Photo 1866.

Library of Congress, Lawrence & Houseworth Collection

The air up there in the clouds is very pure and fine, bracing and delicious. And why shouldn't it be? — it is the same the angels breathe. I think that hardly any amount of fatigue can be gathered together that a man cannot sleep off in one night on the sand by its side. Not under a roof, but under the sky; it seldom or never rains there in the summer time. I know a man who went there to die. But he made a failure of it. He was a skeleton when he came, and could barely stand. He had no appetite, and did nothing but read tracts and reflect on the future. Three months later he was sleeping out of doors regularly, eating all he could hold, three times a day, and chasing game over mountains three thousand feet high for recreation. And he was a skeleton no longer, but weighed part of a ton. This is no fancy sketch, but the truth. His disease was consumption. I confidently commend his experience to other skeletons.

Mark Twain, 1872

California Company's stage leaving the International Hotel in Virginia City headed to California via Donner Lake, 1860s.

So we packed off, crossed a hill, sank into Lake Valley and out of it again, crossed the summit and struck the Placerville road, the grand artery of travel to Washoe. Over it pass the Overland telegraph and the Overland mail. It is stated that five thousand teams are steadily employed in the Washoe trade and other commerce east of the Sierra—not little teams of two horses, but generally of six horses or mules, often as many as eight or ten, carrying loads of three to eight tons, on huge cumbrous wagons. We descended about eight miles and camped at Slippery Ford.

William H. Brewer, 1883

number of persons. The water was perfectly smooth and calm at the time, when suddenly at a locality about two hundred and fifty yards out from shore, was observed to rise in columnar form about five or six feet above the surface of the surrounding water, but soon subsiding and falling down in a whirlpool; this phenomenon being repeated several times—one person rowed out in a small boat and found the water at that spot quite warm. The bed of the lake in the locality surrounding this accident is from thirty to forty feet below the surface of the water, while at the very spot, for a circle of about thirty yards, a hole has been sounded that is at least forty feet deeper, and no fish are to be seen around there, while in former years it has been an excellent fishing ground.

The name of this lake forms a piece of history in itself. The first mentioning of its existence was made by Fremont, who in his report to the chief of topographical engineers, under date of January 10th, 1844, says:

"Beyond a defile between the mountains, descending rapidly about 2,000 feet, and filling up all the lower spaces, was a sheet of green water, some twenty miles broad. It broke upon our eyes like the ocean. The neighboring peaks rose high above us, and we ascended one of them to get a better view. The waves were curling in the breeze, and their dark green color showed it to be a body of deep water. For a long time we sat enjoying the view; for we had become fatigued with mountains, and the free expanse of moving waves was very grateful. It was set like a gem in the mountains, which, from our position, seemed to enclose it almost entirely. Its position at first inclined us to believe it Mary's lake, (sink of Humboldt or Mary's river), but the rugged mountains were so entirely discordant with the description of its low, rushing shores, and open country, that we concluded it some unknown body of water, which it afterwards proved to be. The shore was rocky—a handsome beach, which reminded us of the sea."

Fremont called it "Mountain Lake," and so it was called in California until 1853.

In 1852, the surveyor-general, on a surveying trip for the line of a new wagon road across the Sierras suggested the name of the governor of California, Bigler, for the lake, and this title was conferred upon it by an act of the Legislature of California, in honor of the honest governor, whose reputation—as pure as the water of the lake—never had been smirched by the tongue of scandal. And it became officially and generally known as:

A full team on the Sierras from a Central Pacific Railroad depot. Wagons would carry the goods to their final destination, 1860s.

Library of Congress, Lawrence & Houseworth Collection

There is no end of wholesome medicine in such an experience. That morning we could have whipped ten such people as we were the day before—sick ones at any rate. But the world is slow, and people will go to "water cures" and "movement cures" and to foreign lands for health. Three months of camp life on Lake Tahoe would restore an Egyptian mummy to his pristine vigor, and give him an appetite like an alligator. I do not mean the oldest and driest mummies, of course, but the fresher ones.

Mark Twain, 1872

The stage from Carson arriving at Strawberry Valley, 1860s.

On the morning of November 27th, 1863, as Mr. T. A. Valentine was driving a team on the road between Johnstown and Uniontown he was stopped by a highway man, who demanded his money, at the same time presenting a colt's revolver. Mr. Valentine, being unarmed, handed over his money, amounting to twelve dollars, saying he would much rather part with his money than his scalp. The robber politely assured him that he did not intend to hurt him; he stated to Mr. Valentine that he was strapped and had resorted to robbing to make a raise. He returned Valentine a dollar to pay toll across the Uniontown bridge and a bit to buy a drink, remarking that he never took bits anyhow.

"LAKE BIGLER." Dr. Henry De Groot, in 1859, was exploring the mountains, and gathered at the same time a vocabulary of Indian words, in the Washoe dialect. After him tah-oo-ee means a great deal of water; tah-ve, means snow, and tah-oo means water; and being a writer for the press, he published his explorations in the *Sacramento Union*, suggesting at the same time the word *tah-oo-ee*, as an appropriate name for Lake Bigler, being the Indian term "big water." And when, in 1863, the Rev. T. Starr King and party visited the lake—this was in the time of the rebellion, and Governor Bigler denounced by them as a "copperhead" and secessionist, and therefore unworthy of the honor to dedicate his name to so great a feature of natural scenery, and he (Starr King) appealed himself authority to christen it Lake Tahoe.

California, as well as Nevada Legislatures have repeatedly passed resolutions since that the name of the lake be Lake Bigler, but the name of Tahoe in the mean time had become too much rooted down, that the official declaration could replace it for general use, disposing entirely with the Indian "big water," and now both names are justified, though Lake Tahoe having the greater popularity.

Even a fourth name turned up for some time, and at several times some efforts were made to adopt it officially. A map of this country, published in Europe, was introduced here not infrequently by European immigrants, arriving in early days, particularly those from France, on this map the lake was marked *Bonpland*, called so with Fremont's sanction, by Preuss, the draughtsman accompanying Fremont's party in 1843 and 1844, in honor of Bonpland, a great traveler and geographer accompanying Von Humboldt. All efforts, however, to re-establish the name of Bonpland quieted down without any result.

From McKinney's creek, forming the county boundarie towards Placer, following the shore first south, then in a southeasterly direction to the State line, El dorado has a shore-line on Lake Tahoe—comprising Emerald Bay—of twelve to twenty miles, the State line being resurveyed in 1876, was laid here about half a mile further east. This portion of the lake shore was about the first settled in Lake valley, though the population did not grow in proportion with other parts; the few hotels here, however, are just as well patronized by health and pleasure-seekers from both California and Nevada as those of Tahoe City or Glenbrook. There are the Lake House, Tom Rowland's place;

Eagle Cañon from Eckley's Island, Emerald Bay, Lake Tahoe, 1860s

Most of the teams employed consist of six or eight pairs of mules or oxen, and each team draws two, and sometimes three wagons, attached by chains, and carries from thirty to sixty tons to the load. In regions where there are no roads, they transport timber and fire-wood down the mountains through flumes, constructed of plank, and into which streams of water are conducted, floating the wood and timber, stick by stick, for miles, and going at a rushing rate.

Harvey Rice, 1869

Lake Hotel and Store, Lake Tahoe, California, 1901.

The state built a road that these private companies could transport their materials free over to build their toll road. Now, the tolls on a six-mule team and loaded wagon over the road amount to thirty-two dollars, or thirty-six dollars, I am not certain which sum, and it has paid immensely. In some places the profits during a single year would twice pay the expense of building, repairs, and collection of tolls!

William H. Brewer, 1863

the Tallac House, the property of E. J. Baldwin, (Lucky Baldwin), and the Fishmarket.

The old State Line House, about two miles east of Tom Rowland's place, burnt down in September, 1877, being most pleasantly situated on the lake shore, but its greater curiosity consisted in its location on the State line between California and Nevada; the latter running right through the center of the dining-room, dividing the dining-room table in the middle, making it optional with those taking dinner whether they liked to dine in California or Nevada, or sit in both States at the same time, by taking a seat at the end of the table, the bar being in the State of Nevada.

About half a mile south of McKinney's and only a short distance across over the county line, is another of the curious features of the lake, called the "Georgetown snag." It is a dead tree standing upon its end, having its anchorage in the water at the depth of about 110 feet, rising from six to eight feet above the surface of the water. The usual stand-point of this snag is about 150 yards from shore; but sometimes heavy winds cause it to shift around, yet it never has got far from the spot where first discovered by white men.

As early as 1865 the lake was commenced to be looked at as a water-way, its water became plyed then by two sailing crafts (schooners); but with the increasing influx of summer boarders and tourists the necessity arose to add to the attractions of the lake another new feature, and as a steamer was thought to fulfill the whole programme the best, so a steamer was built and launched, christened *Gov. Stanford*, navigating the lake since the summer of 1873. The *Stanford* is a nice, strong boat, built as a side-wheeler with two decks, in the regularly sound-boat style. Her daily trip runs from Hot Springs to Tahoe City and thence to Glenbrook, whence she takes the direction to Lake Valley, Emerald Bay and Tahoe; these trips connecting with the Central Pacific Railroad on the one side, and the Benton's (Carson) stage (Hank Monk driver) on the other side. The opposition has put in existence a second passenger steamer the *Niagra*; she is a paddle wheeler, like the former, of about the same size, and as her owners have taken the contract for carrying the mail, she is known as the United States mail boat. The *Meteor* is a third boat, built as a propeller, and considered as the fastest boat on the Pacific coast, she is able to make on the lake about twenty-five to twenty-six miles an hour; but she only occasionally attempts to satisfy passenger transportation as she is engaged in the lumber trade.

MINERAL SPRING. GILMORE'S SPRINGS. Mr. Nathan Gilmore is an old El Dorado county man—an early resident of Placerville—since years he is herding cattle and angora goats, of whom he has quite a band pasturing on the shore of Fallen Leaf Lake. Sometimes in 1873, when looking after his cattle between Tallac and Angora Peak his attention was attracted to

At Glenbrook, a lumbering point, the steamer ties up for the night. Here we fully realize that this beautiful lake can be desecrated by practical uses. Logs are made into rafts and floated upon its limped waters; mills are built upon its banks; hard-handed laborers work about its fairy precincts, looking like any thing but angels, although they may become such when they lay off their buff-colored overalls and being baptized in the purifying waters of Tahoe; it may be so, I decline to be their judge.

Caroline M. Churchill, 1881

Steamer on Lake Tahoe, mid 1860s.

The saw mill in the valley of Lake Tahoe, 1860s.

 Upon this lake there is a beautiful little steamer, of sixty-four tons burden, drawing about three feet of water. This boat wears the brand of the Central Pacific Railroad, as nearly everything does upon the Pacific coast, being called the Governor Stanford. At eight o'clock every morning this steamer leaves Hot Spring wharf for Tahoe City and all the points of interest upon the lake.

Caroline M. Churchill, 1881

the foot-tracks of many wild animals all tending in a certain direction, and following the tracks he discovered these springs. There are, as in most every other locality where mineral springs are found, several distinct springs, each discharging a different sort of water. The main spring is reddened all about the edges, with the deposits of iron therein. You watch it, and up from the rocky bottom you see great belchings of gas rising from time to time. These belchings are irregular, and more marked at sometimes than at others. The effect would seem to be the infusion of the waters with their sparkling qualities by those upheavals of gas. This spring flows 200 gallons per hour. An analysis by a skilled chemist shows it to contain these ingredients; carbonic acid, sulphuric acid, seroxid of iron, sodium, bi-carbonate of lime, magnesia, silica, hydrogen gas, organic acids and other things needless to mention. The iron is there in very strong proportions. As a corrective tonic and alternative water, this is found to be a most effective agent.

The other spring seems to be the most promising of the two; its water is almost identical in taste with Congress Water, only more pungent.

Mr. Gilmore has built at his own expense a wagon road from Fallen Leaf Lake to the springs and the drive over from Yank's, is one of the most interesting and satisfactory jaunts a person will undertake and is bound to prove a great attraction to sightseers and tourists as well as to the public in general. The distance from Rowland's to Gilmore's Springs is 10 miles.

Along the shores of Lake Bigler, and far back toward the mountain tops, the timber is being rapidly cleared away, to supply the Virginia mines and the Nevada towns in general. What that annual cut in that region is, we are unable to state. It is run into the lake and towed in rafts by steamers to Glenbrook, whence a narrow-gauge railroad has been built to carry it over the mountains.

The demands of the miners have practically divested the western half of the county of the timber for the manufacture of lumber, but there is no limit to the supply for fuel anywhere, while the new growth will soon cover the vacant lands with all the timber required for any purpose. Further east, excepting the highest peaks of the Sierra Nevada, the country is covered with a dense growth of the finest timber in the world. We believe we are safe in saying that El Dorado county has, to-day, not less than 600 square miles of virgin forests. This consists principally of cedar, spruce, fir, several varieties of yellow pine, and

Placerville Stage going over Carson Pass carrying gold and seven armed guards, 1879.

Steve Crandell Collection, Restoration by Steve Crandell

Clouds of dust arose, filling the air, as we met long trains of ponderous wagons, loaded with merchandise, hay, grain—in fact everything that man or beast uses. We stopped at the Slippery Ford House. Twenty wagons stopped there, driving over a hundred horses or mules—heavy wagons, enormous loads, scarcely any less than three tons. The harness is heavy, often with a steel bow over the hames, in the form of an arch over each horse, and supporting four or five bells, whose chime can be heard at all hours of the day. The wagons drew up on a small level place, the animals were chained to the tongue of the wagon, neighing or braying for their grain.

William H. Brewer, 1863

Sportsman's Hall, was also known as the Twelve-Mile House (12 miles east of Placerville). The hotel operated in the late 1850s and 1860s by John and James Blair. A stopping place for stages and teams of the Comstock, it became a relay station of the central overland Pony Express. At 7:40 a.m., April 4, 1860, Pony Express rider William (Sam) Hamilton, riding in from Placerville, handed the mail to Warren Upson who, two minutes later, sped on his way. The building still stands today in what is now the community of Pollock Pines. Photo, 1865.

On June 30th, 1864, between 9 and 10 o'clock P.M., on the narrow grade about two and a-half miles above Sportsman's Hall, the two coaches of the Pioneer Stage line were stopped by six men, armed with shotguns and pistols, and eight sacks of bullion taken away from them. Ned Blair was driving the first team, Charles Watson the second. Blair was ordered to halt by seizing his leaders and stopping them. They demanded the treasure box, and Blair told them that he had none; whereupon he was ordered to throw out the bullion, and he replied: "Come and get it!" And while two of them covered him with their guns, two others came and took out the bullion. They did not get the treasure box. Blair asked them not to rob the passengers, and they replied that it was not their intention, all that they wanted was the treasure box of Wells, Fargo & Co.

the magnificent sugar pine. In the higher altitudes, tamarack is found in large quantities, while an occasional hemlock puts in an appearance.

During the time when all the freight from Nevada went over the Carson road, teams, on the return trip, loaded with lumber at the mills along that great thoroughfare, for the valleys below. At the present day little is being done in this direction. Complete the Sacramento Railroad to Placerville, and the E. D. W. & D. G. M. Co. will at once find it to their interest to build a V flume from Sportsman's Hall to Placerville. The Main Trunk canal has been constructed with special reference to the transportation of lumber.

In 1897 the Sierra Nevada Lumber & Wood Company built the Hobart Mills complex on Prosser Creek.. They connected it with a seven mile standard gauge railroad that hauled the finished lumber to the Southern Pacific. Dozens of miles of narrow gauge logging railroad were built in the forests north of Hobart Mills. Much of the lumber that built the towns and houses of the interior west came from the Truckee area.

Chapter 9: Truckee to Dutch Flat

TRUCKEE. The name Truckee was given to the home of the leaping trout, the beautiful river that receives its waters from lake Tahoe and carries them swiftly through this enchanting valley, by an emigrant party who slaked their thirst in the cool stream and replenished their nearly exhausted larder from the abundance of its fish. The party passed up the river in the fall of 1844, conducted by the Indian Truckee, or better known as Captain Truckee, whose name was given to this rushing mountain stream.

For years the Truckee basin, however pleasing to the artist's eye, found no favor in the mind of the practical gold seeker. The river yielded not the precious particles so eagerly sought, and was passed by with scarce a thought. Along its banks the Indians contentedly dwelt, and were left undisturbed in their solitude. For a time in 1850 there was an eager rush of gold seekers to Donner lake, caused by the rumored discovery of gold deposits of fabulous richness, but the bubble soon burst and they departed as quickly as they came. Then came the discovery of the celebrated Comstock load in 1859, and the wild rush to the land of silver. Thousands passed through the Truckee basin in the next three years on their way to the Washoe mines. A turnpike road was constructed and a bridge across the Truckee river. The Henness Pass and the Donner lake route both saw the long trains of goods and heard the daily crack of the stage driver's whip. These thousands passed through to the silver land as had the gold seekers a few years before, with no thought of the town soon to spring up on the banks of the clear mountain stream.

The water at the warm springs in the center was poisenous to all kinds of stock, and the road, on the dessert, was lined with dead cattle, mules & horses with here and there a wagon, & all kinds of property in large quantities thrown away. We left no cattle there, but several gave out and laid down when within about six miles of Truckee, & we were obliged to leave our wagons and drive the cattle to water loose.

*Lucius Fairchild
October 13th 1849*

MAD DOG AT TRUCKEE

As Cardwell & Gordon's stage arrived in town from the Summit yesterday, a dog was observed following not far behind, frothing at the mouth profusely. D. W. Bowker and Frank Stevens, both of whom are noted dog fanciers and thoroughly acquainted with the instincts and symptoms of the canine race, saw the animal approaching the express office soon after the stage came, and instantly came to the conclusion that it was afflicted with the hydrophobia. Both of these gentlemen shouted 'mad dog,' and ran, as they supposed, for their lives. The dog also ran after them, and the race was one of the most lively and exciting that has been witnessed in Truckee. Every jump they made they yelled 'mad dog.' The doors of the express office and other buildings were quickly closed, as they naturally would be when a rabid dog was around, and Bowker and Stevens found no place open to give them welcome shelter. All the rest of the people in the vicinity were looking out for their personal safety, and for a minute or two these two men had nothing to do but to dodge and run. They circled around the express office a few times, the dog but a few yards behind, his green eyes gleaming wildly and the froth dropping from his distended jaws.

Continued in right column

Truckee train station, 1870s.

In the year 1863, when the Dutch Flat and Donner Lake wagon road was being constructed across the mountains, Joseph Gray moved here with his family and built a log house. In 1864 J. Jonnell settled on the site now occupied by the Truckee Lumber Co.'s store, the ground being soon after claimed by a man named Owens. The dispute between the two men resulted the shooting of McConnell by Owens. The wounded man recovered and Owens was sentenced to a term of two years in the penitentiary. He [Mr. Coburn] had a log cabin and kept a public house for the accommodation of teamsters and travelers, and a stage station, it being on the line of travel to the Washoe mines. The little place was known as Coburn's Station for several years. When the Central Pacific railroad began to climb the mountains, stations for construction were established along the surveyed route. One of these spots deemed calculated by nature for the site of a town is Coburn's Station, and here a number of people gathered and erected houses, prior to the appearance of the railroad builders. Messrs. Schaffer & Gray built a saw mill just south the present town, and across the river from it, in 1867. In 1868 work commenced upon the railroad at this point, and furnishing lumber and wood for this purpose was the chief business of the place. A great many workmen and railroad employees centered here, and quite a town sprang up at

Coburn's Station, containing five saloons, one large boarding house, three or four stores and a few dwellings. Brickell & Guysendorfer built a water power mill in the immediate vicinity of Coburn's Station, early in 1868. The whole town as destroyed by fire in July, 1868, and Coburn's Station vanished in smoke. A new town was built a little further east, and called Truckee.

Saloons were plenty and gamblers flourished; sporting men and blacklegs collected here, and the place on that account was far from being a paradise.

The year 1871 was one full of trouble for Truckee; three destructive conflagrations visited the town, the last of which nearly sweeping it from existence.

The business of Truckee has been confined to three things, lumber, wood and ice. Millions of feet of lumber have been cut from the surrounding hills, and shipped in all directions. Thousands of cords of wood have been used by the railroad and shipped to consumers far and wide; a great deal of it has been reduced to charcoal and sent abroad in that form. Thousands of tons of purest ice, cut from the frozen waters of the mountain streams, have been stored here in winter, and in summer scattered about the whole coast for the refreshment of the people. Truckee has been and is in the great ice supplying district of the coast. A large round house of a size sufficient to accommodate sixteen engines, was built here after the destruction of the old one in 1869.

Truckee Soda Works, Truckee, California early 1900s.

Steve Crandell Collection, Restoration by Steve Crandell

Continued from left column

The yells of the two men grew weaker under their tremendous exertions. Stevens tried to climb a pine tree in the rear of the express office, but lacked strength through fear and exhaustion, and managed finally to throw himself over the fence in the rear of the kitchen of the Truckee Hotel. This unusual act of Stevens somewhat disconcerted the dog, and after taking a ferocious look through the boards of the fence at the prostrate body, he turned and again made for Bowker. The latter at this critical juncture made a bee line for the front door of the hotel. Constable Getchell, who has taken considerable stock in rabid dogs in his day, and has prescribed for them with success upon diverse occasions, appeared upon the scene of action with a hose, and as the dog came frothing after Bowker, he discharged a powerful stream full in the animal's face. The dog stopped as suddenly as if shot, and seemed grateful for the cooling stream poured upon him. Bowker in the meantime got inside the hotel, and received such assistance as his exhausted condition required.

It seems that the dog had followed the stage from the Summit, and his long run had made him thirsty, causing the frothing at the mouth, and ran after these gentlemen thinking one of them to be his master. They all recovered -- Bowker, Stevens and the dog.

Republican, June 20, 1874

Snow plow of the Central Pacific Railroad near Cisco, 1860s.

We are at an altitude of over six thousand feet, the nights are cold, and the dirty, dusty teamsters sit about the fire in the barroom and tell tales of how this man carried so many hundredweight with so many horses, a story which the rest disbelieve—tall stories of marvelous mules, and bad roads, and dull drivers, of fights at this bad place, where someone would not turn out, etc.—until nine o'clock, when they crawl under their blankets and sleep, to be up at early dawn to attend to their teams.

William H. Brewer, 1860-1864

The American House was built in 1868 and called the Weber House and later the Keiser House. The old American House stood where the Pacific House now stands, but was burned in 1878. Truckee is connected with Tahoe City by a telegraph line, constructed in 1873. In 1878, a line was built to Sierra Valley. Telephones are attached to both of these lines.

It is in summer time that Truckee becomes bustling with life. Hundreds of tourists take stages here for the many points of interest. Lumber and business enterprises are then at the height of activity. Three miles distant from the town is the celebrated Donner lake, a sheet of purest crystal water, lying at the base of tall, forest crowned and overshadowing peaks. Still and beautiful it lies, six thousand feet above the level of the storm tossed ocean.

"601 SIX ZERO ONE" This magic number has caused many a heart to quake with fear, and been the ruling motive for the sudden departure of undesirable citizens for "greener fields and pastures new."

From its advent as a railroad town Truckee became infested with gamblers, blacklegs and ruffians, who added nothing to her wealth, but by their presence and lawless acts detracted from her fair name, retarded her advancement and rendered life and property insecure. During the years 1873 and 1874 the complaints of great lawlessness were frequent and earnest. An organization was finally formed to rid the town of all the undesirable characters. November 19, 1874, five desperadoes received a notice to quit town by four o'clock in the afternoon, signed simply" 601." No time was lost by the notified parties, three of them leaving at once and the other two, George Brown and Harry Howard, departing on the eastward bound train at four o'clock. Others were notified, and some of them failed to heed the warning, and on the night of November 24, 1874, a band of masked men, members of the "601," started out to make an example of them. Passing into a saloon where they expected to find the object of their search, they saw a man in a dark passage way in the rear who seemed as if aiming a pistol at them. He was instantly shot dead, and when brought to light proved to be D. B. Frink, editor of the Republican, and a member of the organization. Mr. Frink was one of the enterprising citizens of Truckee, and had devoted himself to the purification of the place, being one of the foremost in the "601."

Constructing snow sheds, 1860s.

Library of Congress, Lawrence & Houseworth Collection

ARRIVED at the summit of the Sierra Nevada, on the line of the railroad, there are many delightful pedestrian and horseback excursions to be made in various directions. At Summit Valley (which is associated with the relief of the tragically fated Donner emigrants, and is only three miles from Donner Pass) there is an odious saw-mill, which has thinned out the forests; an ugly group of whitewashed houses; a ruined creek, whose waters are like a tan-vat; a big sandy dam across the valley, reared in a vain attempt to make an ice pond; a multitude of dead, blanched trees; and yet this valley is not unlovely.

Benjamin Parke Avery, 1850s

The [Chinese] right of property in women is recognized by them and often defended even against our legal authorities.

Ah Quee, of North San Juan, owned a Mongolian maiden named Sin Moy, who was kidnapped by a countryman and brought to Truckee. She brought with her some trinkets, and Ah Quee procured a warrant for her arrest for larceny, simply as a means of obtaining possession of her again. December 17, 1872, the warrant was placed in the hands of Constable Cross, who with a posse of four or five went to the Chinese quarters and attempted to make the arrest. All Chinatown arose in arms to repel the invaders, and a lively conflict ensued, during which some forty shots were fired. The officers secured their prisoner and retired from the field without harm to themselves. Not so with Ah Quee, for he and another Chinaman were seriously wounded, and several Mongolians received slight injuries. An attempted abduction in the evening of January 3, 1874, resulted in a riot and the wounding of half a dozen of the participating Chinamen.

Central Pacific Railroad at Truckee, 1880s.

Steve Crandell Collection. Restoration by Steve Crandell

About six o'clock on Christmas afternoon he and his father were standing in Frank Rabel's saloon, engaged in conversation with the proprietor, when eight masked men entered, one of whom discharged a load of buckshot into young Spencer's body. Spencer fell to the floor and the men departed, supposing him to be dead. Upon examination eight bullets were found lodged in his arm and shoulder. This was the last public demonstration of the organization, and after that a notice signed "601" was a sure passport out of town. Since this purifying process Truckee has been as quiet and orderly a mountain railroad town as one need ever hope to see.

The last street fight of a character once frequent occurred on the afternoon of February 17, 1875. William Van Orman had married an abandoned woman named Mary Stuart, and failed to support her. She went to Virginia City and returned with William Bell to procure her trunk. As they were passing Jerry Payne's saloon on Front street, they were met by Van Orman, who instantly shot Bell. Five shots were fired by the two men, one of them lodging in Bell's abdomen, and two others in Van Orman's chest and back. Both men recovered from their wounds in time to slip out of town and avoid prosecution as well as the clutches of "601."

"CISCO. Is in the snowy region of the Sierra, fifty-six miles northeast of Auburn, and 5,934 feet above the level of the ocean.

With the opening of the Donner Lake Wagon Road, in 1864, for travel to the silver mines of Nevada, numerous stations, or hotels, were established along its line. Among these were Heaton's and Poley's, a few miles apart. With the rush of people thither the two stations mentioned were points of departure from the Donner Lake Road, and both aspired to be towns. In June the place at Heaton's was surveyed into lots, and the town named Cisco, in honor of John J. Cisco, United States Treasurer. On the 29th of November, 1866, the Central Pacific Railroad was completed and the cars commenced running to this point, and Cisco became a very busy place, crowded with great freight wagons and teams, stages and travelers. This remained the terminus of the road until 1868, when the summit tunnel was completed and the road extended out into Nevada.

DUTCH FLAT. This place is situated in the northeastern part of the county, upon the ridge which divides the waters of Bear River from those of the North Fork of the American, thirty-one miles from Auburn, and dates back in the annals of time to the year 1851.

Teams waiting for freight from the Central Pacific Railroad at Cisco, 1860s.

The telegraph operator told us that Mr. Cook's car had been caught in a snow shed near Summit Station, and had lain there, with the train to which it was attached, more than 40 hours, and had gone on only a few hours before. Dr. Hard stated, afterwards, that had we been in the snow shed in their car, where they could get neither back nor forward, the shed being covered by a mountain of snow, the sick son of the writer would have died in a few hours. Mr. Cook, learning that we were following him so closely, telegraphed back that he would wait for us at Ogden. This was to us a matter of great satisfaction, as the cars we were in were not as comfortable as they ought to have been, and were cold and crowded. Near Summit Station, with the snow piled up to a depth I never saw equaled before anywhere, at 12 o'clock at night, our train ran OFF THE TRACK.

D.L. Phillips, 1876

Well, we struck over the mountains for the Truckee River, to this place, where new mines have "broken out"—at least, a new excitement. We crossed a high volcanic ridge, very rough trail, all the way through an open forest of pines and firs, as one finds everywhere here, and camped on the river about Knoxville. Here I have been examining the "indications" today. Six weeks ago, I hear, there were but two miners here; now there are six hundred in this district. A town is laid off, the place boasts of one or two "hotels," several saloons, a butcher shop, a bakery, clothing stores, hardware and mining tools, etc.—all in about four weeks.

I would give twenty-five dollars for a good photograph of that "street." A trail runs through it, for as yet a wagon has not visited these parts. The buildings spoken of are not four story brick or granite edifices—not one has a floor, not one has a chair or table, except such as could be made on the spot. This shanty, in the shade of a tree, with roof of brush, has a sign out, "Union Clothing Store." I dined today at the "Union Hotel"—a part of the roof was covered with canvas, but most of it with bushes—and so on to the end of the chapter. The crowd— only men (neither women nor children are here yet)—are all working or speculating in "feet."

William H. Brewer, 1860-4

The town of Cisco, Placer County, 1860s

Joseph Doranbach has the honor of being called the first settler, having located there in the spring of that year. The name" Dutch" is derived, perhaps, from the nationality of Mr. Doranbach and those who were his companions at the time, but it is difficult to conceive of why" Flat" should be added in giving the name to the then embryo town, except it is to fully carry out and demonstrate the Californian custom of perverting names. After the completion of the Bradley, or Placer County Canal, from the North Fork of the American, and the Bartlett & Thomas Ditch, from Little Bear River, in 1859 and '60, the town steadily increased, until, in 1860, its voting population was larger than that of any other town in the county, over 500 votes.

This is one of the principal and best-known mining localities of California, the system of hydraulic mining being carried on very extensively. The hill of gravel denominated Dutch Flat is somewhat isolated, presenting three sides to the attack of the hydraulic, and overlooks Bear River, which runs along its northern base, about 1,200 feet below the crest of the hill. Gold is found throughout the gravel, but there is a thick stratum of pipe-clay barren of the precious metal. In this district are a large number of mining companies, and the operations are very extensive and interesting. The Cedar Creek Company, purchasing several properties in 1872, was one of the most extensive. It was an English corporation, with a capital stock of £200,000. During its most prosperous condition, there were 150 men employed.

In 1860, a company was organized to construct a wagon road from Dutch Flat to the eastern slope, to accommodate the travel then beginning to flow over the mountains to the silver mines of Nevada. Two roads were subsequently constructed, and for several years the town profited by the large travel through it. In July, 1866, the Central Pacific Railroad reached the vicinity of the town, and soon passing on, making Cisco the depot of passengers and freight, and business relapsed to its former dependence on the resources of its neighborhood.

Dutch Flat is situated high up in the mountains, its altitude being about 3,400 feet above the sea-level.

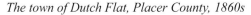

The town of Dutch Flat, Placer County, 1860s

Library of Congress, Lawrence & Houseworth Collection

October 1, 1855, James Freeland, while gambling at Oak Flat with a man called" Greek George," accused the latter of cheating, and a quarrel ensued. During the melee, Freeland picked up a gun standing in the room and killed his antagonist. For this he was tried, condemned, appealed to the Supreme Court where the judgment was affirmed, and on the 6th of June, 1856, was hanged at Auburn. Freeland was a young man, a native of Tennessee; had been a soldier in the Mexican war, and a resident of Placer County since 1850. He claimed to have acted in self-defense, and that the witnesses against him were attacking him when he fired the fatal shot. At his execution he maintained a firm and collected manner without a sign of bravado or braggadocio which elicited the sympathy of the public.

Suspension bridge over Deer Creek, Nevada City, 1860s.

Chapter 10: Nevada City, Grass Valley, Auburn

NEVADA CITY. The county seat and chief city of the county, and for many years the largest and most populous, is Nevada City. Tho' still retaining its prestige as the chief city it has had to give way to Grass Valley in the matter of size and population. It is the terminus of the railroad and in consequence continues to be as it has been for years, the distributing point of supplies for large extent of territory. Upon it the mining camps north and east draw for their supplies and sustenance. From it stages run in all directions and many heavily loaded freight wagons toil

"...as at all these 'diggins,' it isn't the diggers who get the bulk of the gold, but the traders. Think of twelve dollars a dozen, eh! Her husband remained absent about four weeks; and, though he came back with a pretty good 'find,' she, laughed outright at his gold-washing, for her shirt-washing had realized, during the same period, nearly double the value in dollars of the ore he had found."

William Redmond Ryan, 1848-9

One of the most curious instances of juvenile depravity and criminal cunning occurred here recently, worthy of being more fully recorded than this work admits of. For a long time prior to April, 1879, many persons in the city, both male and female, were annoyed by receiving anonymous communications of an obscene character. These were so skillfully delivered that the bearer could not be seen, were shoved under doors, dropped on sidewalks, scattered on the floor during dancing parties, and circulated at public entertainments. Efforts were made to find the perpetrators, but for months they remained undetected. The paper, ink and other materials used were unlike any other to be found, and the handwriting was always the same. The composition showed the author to be possessed of sufficient education to write grammatically. At Hunt's Hall these missives would fly about the room, and the sharpest eyed detectives failed to see from whence they came. Finally it was surmised that they were thrown through the ventilation registers, and an officer secreted himself in the basement during one of these affairs, and while there, a man entered and stepped up to the register. The officer seized him and after a severe struggle succeeded in overpowering him. Upon being brought to a light he proved to be a young man named E. H. Moore

Stage coach crossing the Sierras, late 1800s.

Mead Simpson Collection, Restoration by Steve Crandell

laboriously over the hills, carrying supplies to the mining camps that lie hidden in the recesses of the mountains.

The first time that the eye of a white man ever rested upon or his foot pressed the soil of Nevada City, so far as we can learn, was in the summer of 1848, when James W. Marshall, so widely celebrated as the discoverer of gold at Coloma, while conducting a party of immigrants over the mountain encamped on the banks of Deer creek to spend the night. As was customary upon reaching a stream, after the discovery of gold, Marshall panned out some of the dirt on the bank of the stream and found good "color." What he found, however, did not impress him with the phenomenal richness the stream was afterwards found to contain, and that two years later, within three miles of the spot that witnessed this infant effort, more than ten thousand miners would be at work.

For a number of years ladies, especially of a desirable kind, were in a woeful minority, but now their sweet presence and refining influence are a power in the city for good. Madame Penn came in the fall of 1849; she was an indefatigable worker, taking her turn with her husband in carrying dirt and agitating the rocker.

About the time Caldwell's store was opened John Truesdale built a cabin on Broad street, and, later, a few other cabins were built, and early in the winter canvas tents and brush shanties were erected in great numbers by the miners who were attracted here by the reports of the fabulous richness of the diggings along Deer creek and Gold Run. The place became known, besides the name previously given, as Deer Creek Dry Diggings. The number of miners who wintered here, driven from the rivers by the high water, and awaiting the return of spring to commence operations here in earnest, is not certain, but it was probably in the neighborhood of one thousand. All the winter they kept coming in and as spring began to open they came in large numbers.

By this time several hotels and boarding houses, saloons and stores had been opened. Madame Penn had built a boarding house on the site of the present Union Hotel, John Truesdale had built his board building on Broad street the previous fall. Truex & Blackman had built a log store on Main street. Robert Gordon a large store on Commercial street, and Womack & Kenzie a cloth hotel at the junction of Main and Commercial streets. Besides these there were several cabins and canvas housed, chiefly on Main street, which was the principal and almost the only street in town.

Several small ditches were dug during the year, small now but for those times large enterprises. The Coyote diggings were discovered and the town of Coyoteville sprang up on the lead, just back of Nevada City. As winter approached the merchants

Nevada City, 1852.

The rain came on again last evening, and it has literally poured through the night. The stage—a long wagon came at seven o'clock, and, ourselves included, there were twelve inside. We took a different road through the country, from that by which we came, traversing the side of the mountains and directing our course towards Sacramento. The mountain streams had been swollen by the rains, and in several through which we passed, the water came up to the body of the carriage. Then, too, we were constantly kept on the *qui vive* by the directions of the driver,—"To the right, or the stage will be over!"—"To the left!" etc.—obliging us continually to "trim ship," to the manifest terror of the two ladies within. We passed, every few miles, traces of mining and excavations, or saw long flumes stretching across the landscape. The country is what at the West they call "oak openings," covered with large trees without any under-brush. Occasionally there were large fields under cultivation, where the settler had devoted himself to the certainty of agriculture instead of the lottery of mining.

Right Rev. William Ingraham Kip
Tuesday, 25th. 1892

Coyote and Deer Creek Water Company office near Nevada City, 1850s

One of the many devious ways in which the course of true love can be made to run was illustrated in Grass Valley in 1867-8, showing how by a chance buggy ride a man saved $2,000 and gained a wife. A certain young bachelor of Grass Valley paid his "distresses" to one of the beautiful young ladies so numerous in that grassy vale, and matters were rapidly progressing towards a matrimonial entanglement, when for some reason best known to himself the wooing swain "flew the track." The deserted maiden was a girl of spirit, and she immediately commenced suit for breach of promise to marry. The trial commenced January 11, 1868, and the contest waxed hot for three days, resulting in a verdict for the fair plaintiff, with $2,000 damages.

began to lay in enormous stocks of goods. The winter before had been so severe that transportation was impossible, and goods had been extremely high priced. The population to be supplied being now eight or ten times as great as during the previous winter.

Marriageable young ladies have increased to double the number published in the Golden Era some six months ago, and there is still room for more."

On February 23, 1855, in consequence of the suspension of Adams & Co., there was a run upon Wells, Fargo & Co. The agent paid out all the coin and at two o'clock P. M. closed the doors. The excitement was great but as soon as it was allayed Wells, Fargo & Co. were found to be in good condition.

Although the prediction of the editor was not fully realized, still Nevada took a great stride forward during the year. Telegraphic communication was established with Downieville, mining industries were increased, and the city continued to advance in prosperity until the summer of 1856, when it was almost blotted from existence by the conflagration of July 19, 1856.

On the morning of November 8, 1863, the city was again laid in ruins by flames, but it quickly recuperated. Companies were formed who immediately built the Union Hotel and National Exchange Hotel, new business houses were erected and a new court house, and business soon after reviving, Nevada City recovered from this last blow also.

GRASS VALLEY This beautiful mining city, for a long time the second but now the first in size and importance in Nevada county, lies in a lovely little valley, surrounded by gracefully sloping hills, whose sides are dotted with the hundreds of quartz mines that have made the city so famous and prosperous.

In the month of October, 1848, the foot of a white man first invaded this lovely valley, and trampled upon the luxuriant grass. David Stump, a man named Berry and a third companion came when the news of the discovery of gold reached that region, and arrived on the American river during the summer of 1848. In the fall they started from Placerville, on a prospecting tour north. On Bear river they discovered evidences of crevicing having been done, and so continued their journey north. They found a stream running through a fertile valley, whose luxuriant growth of grass and wild pea-vines refreshed their weary eyes. Here they stopped three weeks, and creviced for gold near where the Eureka and Idaho mines have wrested millions from the stubborn rock. They found gold in large quantities and heavy pieces, but when the first indications of approaching winter

The Court House, Nevada City, 1860s.

Library of Congress, Lawrence & Houseworth Collection

I was present one afternoon, just outside the city limits, and saw with painful satisfaction, as I now remember, Charley Williams (Butcher Bill was the man) whack three of our fellow citizens over the bare back twenty-one to forty strokes, for stealing a neighbor's money. The multitude of disinterested spectators conducted the court. My recollection is that there were no attorney's fees or court charges. I think I never saw justice administered with so little loss of time or at less expense. There was no more stealing in Nevada City until society became more settled and better regulated.

*Hon. Richard
J. Oglesby, 1852*

The party who had engaged me to "come over and attend court," told me during the morning that the "case would not come off," as there was a probability of compromising the difficulty, and my services were not needed. I rejoiced at this wise conclusion of the disputants. I had my faithful nag brought out, and started off in the finest style—having made by the visit, for doing nothing, over $13 clear of all expenses.

I knew the road this time, and Bob seemed glad to get back.

Woa, woa, what's the matter now? Oh! I see, a detachment of Indians are coming, and Bob is frightened; but I patted him on the neck—cordially saluted the Indians—Bob galloped on, and I let him "go ahead" until we reached the halfway house, which was only a temporary tent that could be taken down and put up in forty minutes. Here I gave Robert his dinner, and then resumed my journey. Just at the rise of the first mountain I heard some one call out to me "to stop," and upon looking around I saw a ferocious-looking human biped, who again ordered me to stop. I knew his object, and giving whip and spurs to Bobby, I left the gentleman far behind.

S.M. Schaeffer, 1851

Grass Valley from Cemetery Hill, 1860s.

crossed the sky they departed for the valley, fearing to spend the winter season in the mountains.

Except for these gentlemen no one is known to have visited this valley until 1849, when emigrants came here in search of cattle strayed from their camps on Bear river or Greenhorn creek. Here the cattle were found contentedly feeding and fattening upon the tall and juicy grass that billowed before the breeze and waved in the noonday sun. The place was known to them as the grassy valley from which, when a settlement was made, the road was direct and easy to name Grass Valley.

The earliest actual settlers within the limits of the city appear to have been a party of five emigrants who crossed the plains in 1849 and built a cabin on Badger. Boston Ravine, the point that early became of importance, and was the chief settlement in this vicinity for two years.

Quite a number of people mined in Boston Ravine during the fall and winter, and in the spring of 1850 a great many more came, and the settlement began to assume the appearance of a town. By this time Rough and Ready and Nevada had become quite extensive and noted mining camps, and the few scattered settlers of Grass Valley changed the name of the embryo city to Centreville, as it lay midway between those populous locations.

During the summer that part of the valley east of Auburn street was fenced in with brush by some parties, who sold it during the summer to A. P. Willey and a man named McClintock. These gentlemen flattered themselves that they had a "good thing," as hay was eighty dollars per ton, and they could cut two heavy crops a year. Before they had fairly begun to improve the place, some miners wandered into the enclosure, sank a shaft through the rich, black soil, and came to a gravel deposit which proved to be very rich with gold. In less than twenty-four hours the whole ranch was staked off in claims fifty feet square, leaving not even a fifty foot claim for the ravaged proprietors.

In 1851 Grass Valley made rapid strides forward, taking a prominent place among the mining towns of the county. The county was organized that year, but Nevada City had so far outstripped this place in 1850, that she secured the county seat, which she has succeeded in retaining, although Grass Valley now leads her in wealth, business and population.

The early society of Grass Valley was composed of the same incongruous elements that formed the component parts of the a population of every mining camp. Every race, every nation, every religion had its representatives here. A more cosmopolitan collection could not well be imagined, and yet the American element predominated, American customs and institutions prevailed, and it was but a few years before the conglom-

The pack mule was quite heavily laden with the precious cargo. The day was exceedingly pleasant as the little cavalcade marched out of the foot-hills, towards Sutter's Fort. An unpeopled wilderness extended on all sides. No person was met or seen, and as the day wore on, the party became careless and tired. While thus riding and approaching a grove of trees where they thought of camping for the night, the mule and treasure considerably in advance, there rang from the grove a shot and the leader of the mule fell from the saddle. A quick charge, the twirling of a couple of lassoes, and the riderless horse and gold-laden mule were in the possession of a party of four or five Mexicans and under whip and spur were flying toward the Rio de los Americanos.

Miners working Near Sugar Loaf Hill, 1852.

Courtesy of the California History Room, California State Library, Sacramento, CA

Saw mill on the Bear River near Colfax, 1865.

Upon October 11, 1870, [in Nevada City] the ill-feeling existing between two factions of Chinese culminated in a general battle between them. Over one hundred wrathful Celestials, armed with knives, pikes, bars of iron and clubs, mingled their Mongolian imprecations in one general babel of yells and rushed upon each other. Extermination was in their eyes and "hi-yahs" on their lips. The Sheriff instantly organized a posse and quelled the riot, arresting some twenty-five of the Chinamen. No one was killed, but several of the combatants received severe wounds during the affray.

eration became thoroughly Americanized. Saloons abounded and the omnipresent gaming table, behind which sat the ubiquitous and skillful gambler, was ever the center of attraction.

COLFAX. This place is situated on the Central Pacific Railroad, fifty-four miles from Sacramento and eighteen miles northeast of Auburn, and is another of the many towns that sprang into existence upon the completion of the great overland railroad. The rails reached Colfax September 1, 1865, and regular trains were running on the 4th of that month. The town of Colfax was laid out in 1865 by the Central Pacific Railroad Company.

Within half a mile of where Colfax now stands is the old settlement of Illinoistown, and when Colfax was laid out in 1865 it gathered to itself all that was left of this ancient place. Colfax has, since that time, steadily increased in population and importance, until now it is one of the leading towns in the county.

In 1874 a company was formed to build a narrow gauge railroad from Colfax to Nevada City. The work of construction began in 1875, and the road was completed and the last spike driven at Nevada on the 20th of May, 1876.

Rich veins of quartz were discovered near Colfax in 1866. A test of the rock was made at Grass Valley, and found to be worth between $27 and $28 per ton. A company was organized and a mill constructed in 1869. The mine was christened the "Rising Sun." The gold is of a pure quality, being worth $18.50 per ounce. The mill had five stamps of 800 pounds each, and was capable of reducing ten tons per day. The mill was subsequently increased to twenty stamps, and still continues a paying mine.

AUBURN. Auburn the county seat and principal town of Placer County, is on the line of the Central Pacific Railroad, thirty-six miles northeast of Sacramento, the depot having an elevation of 1,360 feet above tide water, the principal portion of the village being forty or fifty feet lower.

The history of Placer County is so much the history of Auburn that a special reference may appear superfluous. The town antedates the county some years, the gold-digger having sought its hidden wealth as early as 1848. The first, however, that it bore a habitation and a name was early in 1849, when it was called the "North Fork Dry Diggings," the name of Auburn being given in the fall.

Hoisting works of the Bullion Mine, Gold Hill

After considerable trouble and delay Mr. Avery again reached Deer creek with one companion, E. Franchere, in February, 1850. He continues : "To my intense disgust I found that my ravine was occupied from one end to another by long-haired Missourians, who were taking out their 'piles.' They worked in the stormiest weather, standing in the yellow mud to shovel dirt into cradle or tom; one of them had stretched a canvas awning over their claims, which were only thirty feet along the ravine. All the other ravines leading into the flat at the foot of American Hill were occupied almost as thickly. At night the [miners] tents shone through the pines like great transparencies, and the sound of laughter, shouting, fiddling and singing startled those old primeval solitudes strangely. It was a wild, wonderful scene. Gambling, of course, was common and fatal affrays were frequent.

Benjamin Parke Avery, 1850

Placer Mining, panning out, 1860s

LEAVING Colfax by the freight train, I find myself once more passing through the Central Pacific's lengthy snow sheds. With the return of spring portions of these structures are removed in order to prevent the spread of fire, and the builders seem to have made use of a variety of plans, as no two tiers of shedding appear to be constructed after the same. In passing one plan of construction, the sun comes pouring through a thousand apertures, striking the train while in motion, giving it the appearance of being showered with golden sun balls, sparkling like falling rockets. In another plan the sun strikes the train in a rapidly moving checkerboard, and the effect is really quite wonderful and very pleasing.

Caroline M. Nichols Churchill, 1881

The locality is a concentration of small gulches, or ravines, constituting a larger one, flowing almost due west into the Sacramento Valley, where the water is lost in the plain. These ravines were rich in gold, and upon the site of Auburn many miners, in the summer of 1849, pitched their tents, and with pans, crevicing knives and spoons, and rockers, dug for the precious metal. Cabins were constructed as pleased the builders' fancy, and when pack-animals and wagons subsequently came they sought their passage way as most convenient, and thus marked out the streets of the future town, resulting in a picturesque irregularity.

The existence of gold in the ravines had been proven in 1848, and the centrality of Auburn, its accessibility, and its proximity to the North Fork, pointed it out as a good trading-point and a good place to pass the winter. Several stores were opened in the summer of 1849, and then stores comprised all business houses in the mines being saloon, eating, gambling, and lodging-house. For cooking and lodging, the miner or traveler usually depended on his own resources, seldom troubling any store or other house for accommodation.

Auburn was then fixed as a trading center, and has so continued. As a town of 1849 it was composed of tents, cloth-houses and log-cabins, with canvas roofs, and in a few instances where roofs made of shakes split from the pine trees which were abundant in the neighborhood. In the summer of 1850 more pretentious buildings were constructed, and frames, and clap-boards, and paint, and plank floors made their appearance.

During its history Auburn has experienced many vicissi-tudes; business, in its first decade, fluctuating with the success and movements of the miners, but with the development of the varied resources of the county greater stability marks its pros-perity.

GREAT FIRES. Several times fire has swept its streets of buildings and hard-earned fortunes from its citizens, but "Re-surgam" has been its motto, and a handsomer village than before has followed each conflagration.

The first and most destructive occurred on June 4, 1855. With characteristic energy the town was rebuilt larger and more substantial than before, only to meet a like fate on the 9th of October, 1859. The fire originated in a small frame building, two doors south of the American Hotel, occupied by some col-

Ladies were in such an overwhelming minority that, at first, their influence was scarcely felt, and ladies of a marriageable age were "scarcer than hens' teeth." A gentleman who took up his residence here in 1852, recently remarked, "When I came here there were only two girls in the town, and one of them was engaged, so I had to take the other. You see," said he, with a smile, "that it was a clear case of Hobson's choice."

Hydraulic Mining behind the pipes in the Kennebec Claim, Birchville, Nevada County, 1860s

Evening view on the American River below Cape Horn (near Colfax), 1860s

MONDAY morning, August 31, I was up at half-past two and took the stage, and was far down the foothills before sunrise, breathing clouds of dust. You can have no idea of the dust of these roads in the dry season. I took breakfast at Auburn, then staged six miles farther, where I took the cars.

William H. Brewer, 1860-4

ored men as a restaurant. From the place where first seen, the fire spread rapidly on all sides, enveloping building after building in rapid succession, and driving their inmates forth in haste. But few minutes elapsed before both sides of the street were in flames, which then ran north and south with a fury that seemed to threaten the total annihilation of the town, but fortunately the walls of the brick houses proved bulwarks that broke the force of the storm, and enabled the citizens to make a successful fight against further destruction.

In the article of the 28th of April, he [the editor of the newspaper the *Auburn Whig*] says: "One great peril necessarily incurred in a thickly-built town or village, is that of conflagration, a danger to which, by reason of our numerous Chinese population, we are particularly liable. *The extremely loose and careless customs of that people are too generally known and understood to require any comment from us, and it is for them in a great measure that we have reason for apprehension.*"

The words in italic seem almost prophetic, where we recall the fact that on the 4th of June following, the fire which laid our village in ashes originated in one of the dens of that tribe.

We will just call attention to the streets in front of the Orleans, and Wells, Fargo & Co's Express office, in verification of this extract, at the present time. Here, we are the center of an extensive stage travel, strangers visiting us daily; the county seat of a large county, the entertainers of our fellow-citizens from all parts of the county attending upon the Courts, and drawn here from their necessities in other matters connected with a county seat, and yet we have none but miry streets without crossings or a system of sidewalks for them to walk upon.

A RAILROAD TOWN. From a very early date, Auburn aspired to be a railroad center, and large sums of money were expended in advocating and assisting such enterprises. From 1852 to 1860, the subject was kept before the people. While incorporated, the town, June 4, 1860, voted a subsidy of $50,000 to the Sacramento, Placer and Nevada Railroad, and succeeded in having a line constructed to within five miles of the town, the history of which is elsewhere given. Auburn depot was established at the terminus, and several lines of stages connected the depot with the town by frequent trips. A large

Mining didn't end when the Gold "Rush" ended. This early 1911 or 12 photo shows miners in the water under the bridge. Note the buildings near the bridge (now known as "No Hands Bridge"). In the early days of bridge construction there was a saloon located there to serve the miners. The bridge workers often took advantage of its availability and were frequently inebriated at work. The builders were forced to purchase the saloon and tear it down so workers could complete the bridge. The bridge in the foreground was one of the predecessors of the current Highway 49 bridge that crosses the American River just below the confluence of the middle and south forks.

The mules seemed to tire and were getting thin, so we concluded to lighten up our load. We did so by cutting a foot off of each wagon, except the sheet iron ones. We thought we had a surplus amount of provisions to take us through, knowing that we would have plenty when we go out there. We couldn't sell our surplus, as we thought, and we piled it up on the roadside, good provisions, flour, bacon and other things, leaving it for the Indians, coyotes or the emigrants who needed provisions.

Edward Washington McIlhany,
1849

Library of Congress.

Ox or mule teams were generally used to move logs out of the deep forest. Starting in the mid 1850s when sections of the rail systems were completed, the logs would often be transferred to a rail car for the rest of their trip.

SEPTEMBER, 1851.

I was solicited "to come over [to Auburn]," state before the "learned court" what I knew, and that my entire expenses would be paid, and I also receive the usual fees "made and provided," etc.

Having no very urgent business to detain me, and in humor for a jaunt, I hired John the baker's favorite nag Bob, and started at a fine pace. I had never traveled over that road before. I hardly knew whether I was going right or wrong. I saw in the almost hidden path no person or living thing, but snakes, tule and luxuriant growing grass, and between Bob and myself, I thought I had lost my way; however, I whipped up Bobby, and kept on a straight course "due south," until I overtook a man standing like a statue beneath the friendly sheltering branches of a large tree. I inquired the route to Auburn, etc.; he replied, "all right—keep right straight on."

Away I galloped, but I stopped again; now there were two paths, and which was the "straight on" one I was puzzled to know, so I halted awhile; soon a traveler came along, and I asked his assistance. He said: "take that path; bad road, sir; hurry up—better not let night overtake you,"

continued in far right column

amount of freight and travel was thus brought through Auburn, giving it a lively appearance and a profitable business. But this, Auburn's railroad and hope, was of short life. A greater railroad, with a more direct and practicable route, approached from Sacramento and absorbed its business. This was the Central Pacific, which was completed to Auburn and commenced running to the present depot, on the southern border of the village, on the 22d of May, 1865. The hope had been entertained that the railroad would pass through the center of the town, but this being impracticable, all became satisfied with the location, and Auburn congratulated itself upon being most happily situated. Among the institutions of Auburn was the California Stage Company.

DAMASCUS. Damascus is an old mining town, whose history begins in the year 1852, at which time Dr. D. W. Strong, who was prospecting in the vicinity, discovered gold in an outbreaking stratum of quartz gravel upon a point between the two branches of Humbug Cañon, near the southern, or as it is now called, Damascus Branch.

During the inclement season, in cases of sickness, no little difficulty is experienced in procuring the attendance of a physician, the nearest one residing some ten miles & distant, at Iowa Hill. At one time, during the prevalence of a fierce snow-storm, and when the earth was enveloped to the depth of many feet, it was found after nightfall that a lady resident, the wife of a miner, was suffering with an attack of pneumonia, and, without relief, could not long survive. Females were never at any time numerous in the camp, but those who were there were respectable ones, and were all favorites with the male population. A physician must be had at every hazard; work in the tunnels for that night, at least, was abandoned; twenty brave men assembled, who, under the leadership of Gould Coker, set out in the gloom of night, in the blinding storm, to break a trail to Iowa Hill for the physician. By turns, each man would take the lead in the deep snow until exhausted, and another took his place, as, waist deep, they wallowed slowly onward through the cold, fleecy mass. Some time upon the following day the heroic little party reached Iowa Hill, and, after prevailing upon Dr. O. H. Petterson to accompany them, started upon the homeward journey. This trip, though not as fatiguing as the one out, was in itself no child's play; for, meanwhile, the storm continued to rage, and the fast-falling snow had well-nigh obliterated the trail previously made. But perseverance, at length, overcame every obstacle, and within thirty-six hours from the time of starting for the doctor, he was at the bedside of the suffering woman, and not too late to save her life. When the patient was past danger, the humane miners were again obliged to escort the doctor home, breaking the road much after the manner they had been compelled to do at first.

Miner's log cabin, 1852.

continued from far left column

It occurred to me that his advice coincided with the information a friend had imparted, relative to a suspicious house midway. Now, I am not a nervous man, nor am I a fighting man, but I observed the strictest watch, for I well knew that lawless and vicious men were prowling around. On—on I spurred my faithful nag.

I never carried a pistol in my life; I never assaulted anyone. As soon as I emerged from the rank, men came towards me, and offered inducements for me to alight, but my business was urgent, my horse was restless, and away I galloped.

At the summit of the mountain I found the "traveler's rest"—a shingle hut. The landlord told me I could reach Auburn before dark. I mounted Bobby. I overtook a solitary miner, who informed me that "when I rounded yonder hill, Auburn would not be a mile off."

Thanking him, I spurred up Bob, and thought of that lone miner— perhaps he was working for the support of aged parents; perhaps for the successful accomplishment of some cherished object; but hark! I hear yells and a loud noise. Bobby snorted and galloped faster; we "rounded yonder hill," and looking down the valley, I saw Auburn below us.

S.M. Schaeffer, 1851

Westwood Stage Line carrying 28 passengers in Greenville 1800s

I prospected with good success in a claim that had just been abandoned by the notorious Greenwood, carrying dirt in a pan to a dug-out cradle. Went with shovel and pan seven or eight miles up the creek, testing several ravines as high up as the top of the ridges, seldom, in my ignorance, going deeper than a few inches, and always getting gold. A preacher, whose name I forget, was then hauling dirt from one big ravine back of Caldwell's on an ox cart, and washing it at the creek with good success. A few other men were carrying dirt from other ravines on their own backs or those of mules.

Benjamin Parke Avery, 1849

DEADWOOD. Deadwood is situated about seven miles above Michigan Bluff, across El Dorado Cañon, on the divide between that stream and the North Fork of the Middle Fork.

Periodically during winter come fearful storms of rain and snow in these high altitudes. An occasional avalanche is loosened from near the summit's crest, which sweeps everything before it. In December, 1860, on one side of the hill, about one-fourth of a mile below the village stood the house of A. J. Felch, occupied by himself, wife, and boy, aged eight, named William. On Christmas eve, while father and son were sitting in the house before a comfortable fire (Mrs. Felch fortunately being absent), all at once the roar which precedes the approaching landslide smote upon their ears. Before it was possible to get out of doors, the avalanche struck the building, and crash! it went, apparently carrying away inmates and all! Not so, however, for soon Mr. Felch became conscious that he was still alive ! though cut, bruised, and bleeding from contact with falling timbers. But where was the boy? A plaintive call from the father elicited no response. Dead, mangled and swept away into the fierce-raging chasm below ! thought the poor, wounded, agonized father; but he would search for the lost one. Providentially, some oak trees to which portions of the building had been attached had withstood the onslaught of the moving mass, and, under the protecting lee of these, there yet remained debris of the household wreck. Digging among this the father found his boy, unharmed. That either escaped, is little less than a miracle.

LINCOLN Is situated in the valley of the Sacramento, bordering the foot-hills of the Sierra Nevada, near where Auburn Ravine debouches upon the plain. It is on the line of the California and Oregon Railroad. The place was named in honor of Charles Lincoln Wilson, the builder of the California Central Railroad, which was completed to this point October 31, 1861. In the years 1862-63, the town was very prosperous, having at that time between 400 and 500 inhabitants, and from four to eight stages making daily trips from Lincoln.

The Lincoln Winery, was established in 1880, by Stephen D. Burdge, who learned the business of wine-making in Italy.

The Clipper Coal Mine was discovered in June, 1874, by J. D. B. Cook. In March. 1875, Mr. Gladding, the senior member of the firm of Gladding, McBean & Co., the present owners of the pottery, being on this coast, took some of the clay found in the Lincoln coal mine to Chicago. The sample proved suitable for sewer pipe and on that class of goods; a company was soon formed. About thirty-five men and boys are employed constantly; the principal manufacture is sewer pipe, but in connection with this they make well-pipes, chimney-tops, flower-pots, lawn-vases, and ornaments of all descriptions.

ROGERS' SHED. The "Shed," or "Union Shed," as afterwards called, was built by E. C. Rogers, in December, 1857, and comprised a one-story house, 24x80 feet, and the uninclosed shed in front, 40x40 feet, and twenty feet high, under

...the avalanche struck the building, and crash ! it went, apparently carrying away inmates and all!

Stage Line in Marysville, 1880s

Mountain Stage on quarry road in Auburn Ravine, 1860s.

"My Dear Wife,

...there are thousands here now, to say nothing of thousands on the way, that will not earn enough above their expenses to carry themselves home, during a years residence. For a man must eat, whether he lays up any thing or not My own expenses in my own cabin, and doing my own cooking, are equal to the expense at a first class hotel in the states It averages about 1 1/2 dollars pr day.

E. A. Spooner,
California April 21st
1850

the shelter of which the monstrous freight teams, then thronging the roads, could repose, and be sheltered from summer's heat or from the winter's rain. A large barn and corral were also an attachment of the premises upon the opposite side of the road. Situated as the "Shed" was upon the old Sacramento and Nevada road, and there being also four other roads diverging there-from, it became, in those early days, quite a noted place. For four or five years after its establishment, two stages passed the "Shed" daily; and the number of big freight teams during that period was from forty to sixty each day.

SHIRT-TAIL CAÑON. On the North Fork of the American River Shirt-tail Cañon presents itself, to the beholder. The unique name it bears was bestowed in the following manner: Early in the summer of 1849 two men were prospecting — they emerged [at a] bend in the creek a short distance below them [that] obstructed the view. Abruptly turning the point, they were astonished to see before them, a solitary individual engaged in primitive mining operations. The apparition was perfectly nude, with the exception of a shirt, and that was not overly lengthy. The lone miner was in the edge of the water, and, happening to look up at about the same time that they discovered him. Had this not been so, they declared afterward, would have stepped back, made some noise, and given the man a chance to don his overalls. As it was, the eyes of both parties met, and an involuntary "hello!" came from all three mouths. "What in the devil's name do you call this place?" queried one of the intruders of the *sans cullottes*. He glanced at his bare legs, and from them to his questioners, took in at a moment the ludicrous appearance he made, and laughingly answered: "Don't know any name for it yet, but we might as well call it Shirttail as anything else," and under that euphoneous nomenclature has it since been known, and must thus go down to posterity.

FOREST HILL. This mining town is pleasantly situated on the ridge between Shirt-tail Cañon and the Middle Fork of the American River, at an elevation of 3,230 feet above the sea. The point being well situated for trade, it was occupied in the fall of that year by M. and James Fannan and R. S. Johnson, who established a trading-post. This wayside brush shanty grew into a house and hotel, known as the Forest House, as here was a dense forest of pine, fir, spruce, and oak trees. In 1851 other houses were built in the vicinity, and the Forest House became quite an important trade and travel center.

Mining was continued in a small way in the neighboring gulches, but an accident in the winter of 1852-53 led to greater enterprise and the opening of the deep mines which have given to Forest Hill its celebrity. That winter is historically remembered as one of great severity of storm and flood. During one of the storms a mass of earth was loosened at the head of Jenny Lind Cañon. Upon going to their claim, when the storm had abated, they saw with dismay the havoc that had been wrought.

Miner and his donkeys, perhaps in search of a new claim.

October 20, 1853, an atrocious murder was committed near a house called "Traveler's Rest," in Auburn. Andrew King, a quiet and peaceable young man, had refused to lend three dollars to Robert Scott at a gaming-table on the evening of the 19th. The next day Scott called King out of his house and, presenting two loaded revolvers, told King to take one and defend himself. This the latter refused and turned to go into the house, when Scott fired and instantly killed his victim.

The murderer fled, but was later arrested. In due time Scott was brought to trial, and was convicted and sentenced by Judge Howell to be hanged on the 31st of March, 1854.

On the day of the execution, a large number of people assembled at Auburn from all parts of the county to witness the appalling sight of launching a fellow-being into eternity through the dread process of the law.

Miners working in Gold Run, 1800s.

"I started from Mormon Island on a prospecting trip to <u>Reading Springs</u> (<u>Shasta</u>), in October, 1849. Rode a little white mule along with pork and hard bread and blankets packed behind me. On the way from Sacramento to Vernon, a trading station just started at the junction of the Sacramento and Feather rivers, I encountered a party on horse back who were coming from Deer creek, and who told me big stories about 'pound digging;' in Gold Run. As 'pound diggings,' i.e. claims that would yield twelve ounces of gold per day to the man, were just what I was in search of.

Benjamin Parke Avery, 1849

A great slide of earth had covered their mine and mining implements, and, in curiosity, they proceeded to examine the mass and the freshly-rent bank whence it came, and it was a bank of rich deposit for them. Chunks of gold were seen glistening in the gravel, and these they at once proceeded to gather, finding some $2,000 or $2,500 worth a day. This led to the opening of the Jenny Lind Mine, which has produced over $1,100,000 of gold.

GOLD RUN. Is situated on the line of the Central Pacific Railroad, twenty-nine miles northeast of Auburn, having an elevation above the sea of 3,206 feet. Mr. Brown, who had been a banker at Gold Run, stated that there had been shipped, through Wells, Fargo & Co.'s Express, from 1865 to 1878, $4,500,000.

MICHIGAN BLUFF. The work done in that vicinity during the year 1849, seems to have been confined entirely to the bars upon the adjoining streams in the deep cañons, and this was only in the shallow places, by crevicing. That fall two men being at work upon the Middle Fork of the American, decided to follow up the stream and in doing so they reached the mouth of a large cañon coming into the river from the northeast, where they found in crevicing the cleanly water-washed bed-rock, considerable quantities of large, heavy gold. Not long after this the rainy season begun and they were compelled to leave-going to Pilot Hill, El Dorado County, where, during; the summer, they had located claims to be worked in the winter after water came.

While at Pilot Hill they exhibited their gold to a number of persons, whom they informed of their intention to return in the spring to the spot where they obtained it, but only to their intimate friends would they disclose the locality. Quite a company of men thus became interested in the prospect between the friends of all — some of whom were living at Coloma, some at Hangtown, and at other places-to the number of twenty or twenty-five. Outside of this particular circle nobody new where the good diggings of the Bronsons were located. It nevertheless became notorious that they were to start out in the spring, and parties were constantly on the watch prepared to follow them up. Meanwhile the favored ones were going well provided for; they had purchased not less than sixty mules and horses, and packed to the rendezvous at Pilot Hill. February was a pleasant month; the continued fine weather brought out the early vegetation and flowers, so that by the middle of that month the party thought the season far enough advanced to justify a movement. Accordingly, with as much secrecy as any such large party could gather, they assembled, packed up and went away at night. Not many days elapsed after the cavalcade had got under

The crowning act of [Rattlesnake Dick's] gang, was the robbery of Wells, Fargo & Co.'s gold train from Yreka. Dick and his men had previously ascertained that the bullion, amounting to $80,000, would be packed on mules, guarded by twenty men, and driven, by way of Trinity Mountain, and it was at this place they resolved to attack the train.

They carried away with them about $40,000 worth of the gold, and buried the remainder in the mountain. They carried the gold to their rendezvous at Folsom. In the meantime, the party of twenty men tied up on Trinity Mountain managed to cut loose, and hurrying into the lower country, gave information of the robbery to the authorities. A fearful hue and cry was immediately raised against the daring robbers, and Jack Barkley, then Wells & Fargo's detective, started in pursuit of the highwaymen. The opposing parties met at night near Folsom, and the firing commenced on both sides. For a few moments the affray was very hot, Barkley shooting a way from two revolvers, and his companion firing at every opportunity. Carter [one of the robbers] was afterward pardoned for certain information which he gave the detectives in regard to the stolen property, and which led to the ultimate recovery of the $40,000 concealed in the "den" at Folsom.

Construction of the Bayley House began in 1861, after A.J. Bayley's first hotel in Pilot Hill, the Oak Valley House, burned. Prompted by rumors that the Central Pacific Railroad would be built through Pilot Hill, Bayley started construction. He had every reason to believe that the railroad would be routed through the trail that John C. Fremont surveyed, which ran past his property, because it had already been established as a freight haulers' route. Theodore Judah found that routing the railroad through Auburn and Dutch Flat would be less expensive, leaving Bayley with a massive, Southern style estate in Pilot Hill, El Dorado County.

This mine shaft in the Southern Mines in Los Floriez Cañon is similar to the mining done in the Pilot Hill mine as well as the Hunt mine near Hoggs Diggings, about four miles north of Pilot Hill.

Pilot Hill presents one of the most characteristic pictures of feverish mining life. In the summer of 1850 several sailors first discovered gold there, in the dark ravines, and at the bends of the main valley. Platinum was found in pieces as large as an ounce but ignorant miners, thinking it to be another metal of no value, threw it away. Thus one of these men once presented me with a pretty specimen of it. Soon a town of about thirty houses was built and it was thought that by the end of the year it would double in size. Three months later the region was again wilderness.

Carl Meyer, 1855

way, before there were from 500 to 600 men in their wake-pursuing them, and as rolling snow gathers volume as it courses down an inclination, so did the crowd of pursuers increase as it proceeded, until the rush became enormous.

OPHIR. The name of Ophir was a favorite one with the pioneer gold-hunters, and it was given to numerous localities and claims which were supposed to be of extraordinary richness. Here was supposed to be the land of Ophir spoken of in the Bible, whence came the gold to adorn the temple of Solomon. The Ophir of Placer County is situated on Auburn Ravine, about three miles west of the Court House. In 1852, it was the most populous town in the county.

PENRYN. The busy town of Penryn bases its prosperity upon the enduring granite, and a more solid and lasting foundation could not be found or desired. The site is on the line of the Central Pacific Railroad, eight miles southeast of Auburn. The town is a growth of the granite quarries in the neighborhood, which were opened in 1864. This was not at once made a station, and passengers to and from Penhryn-as it was then spelled, were obliged to go to some other station. Later a station was established, and the spelling of the name changed to suit the modern method of simplicity. Penryn owes its existence and prosperity as a town to Griffith Griffith, the proprietor of the celebrated Penryn granite quarries.

ROCKLIN. This is a thriving village on the line of the Central Pacific Railroad, fourteen miles southwest of Auburn. Here is a round-house of the Central Pacific Railroad, where the extra locomotives are kept which are necessary to attach to trains ascending the mountain. Here also are large granite quarries, giving employment to many people. The water supply of the railroad company is brought a distance of six or seven miles, from Secret Ravine. Well water is used for animals and many domestic purposes, but all the drinking-water is furnished free by the railroad company, from Blue Cañon. Not a Chinaman is to be found at Rocklin. The roundhouse is capable of accommodating about thirty engines. A great deal of wood is consumed by engines, there sometimes being as much as 25,000 cords piled there at once.

ROSEVILLE. The railroad name of this place is Junction, as here the Oregon Division joins the Central Pacific. It is eighteen miles southeast of Auburn. The town plat was laid out in 1864. Cyrus Taylor was the first resident; Van Trees built the first hotel, and W. A. Thomas opened the first store. A good farming and grazing region surrounds the town, giving it a substantial and increasing business. The name is derived from the neighboring ranch of Rose Spring.

END

Originally the McLaglen Store, then the Nance Store & Bar at Pilot Hill, late 1800s.

Library of Congress

The stories we heard in regard to the richness of the mines were very much exagerated, still they are very rich & a man by hard work and great perseverance can make a fortune in a few years. Some make large fortunes in a few days but on the other hand some do not hardly pay their board. You can rely on my being satisfied with a small pile as I am very anctious to return home, & when there I will be perfectly contented and I advise all of my friends, & everybody, if they have food & clothes in the States never to come to this country, but be satisfied where they are, but above all, never come the land route for God's sake.

Lucius Fairchild
October 13th 1849

It is now a stirring mining town, surrounded by extensive diggins; but let the mines give out or better ones be discovered five miles distant, this would soon be "the deserted village." As we left the town, we passed through a street inhabited entirely by Chinese, who are to be met with in all parts of the mines.

Descending into the plain below, we had magnificent views of the Valley of the Sacramento which stretched far as the eye could reach, seeming to be an unbroken expanse of forest land. The sun was shining brightly, and every pleasant little nook we passed appeared to be occupied by miners. Sometimes there was a neat cabin, as if the occupant had made up his mind to a long residence, but generally there were only canvas tents. They looked so pleasant, however, this bright afternoon, the men working in the gulches, that a passer-by would imagine mining to be a most agreeable employment.

Right Rev. William Ingraham Kip
Tuesday, 25th. 1892

Hauling sluice boxes from the Blue Gravel Claim in Smartsville, Nevada County, 1800s.

Epilogue

Even though the Gold Rush had been officially over for many years, more than 100 million dollars worth of the glittery mineral came out of the area's rivers in the early part of the 20th century.

By then, the Golden State's economy had turned to agriculture as its primary industry. As the 20th century progressed, California's "gold" shifted to other industries including canning, banking, motion pictures and aerospace. With war, ship building and aviation became profitable and attracted scientists from around the world. As defense spending waned, the high-tech industry emerged, creating California's new "gold."

A mere 150 years after the Gold Rush, California now boasts a population in excess of 35 million and is still growing.

So enjoy California's great heritage, its diversity, and its incredible beauty. And the next time you travel *The Golden Corridor* remember that it's paved with the blood, sweat and tears of the pioneers who settled this great state.

Bibliography

Books, Journals and Experts

Annals of San Francisco. Frank Soulé, John H. Gihon, James Nisbet, 1855

History of Placer County California. Thompson & West, 1882

Historical Souvenir of El Dorado County California. Paolo Sioli, 1883

History of Sacramento County. Thompson & West, 1880

History of Nevada County. Thompson & West, 1880

Voyage to California. Lucy Kendall Herrick, Huntington Library Press, 1998

On the Winds of Destiny. Jacqueline Lewin & Marilyn Taylor. Platte Purchase Publishers/St. Joseph Museum, Inc., 2002

California Archaeology. Michael J. Moratto. Academic Press, Inc., 1984.

Leakey Foundation, Dr. Alan Almquist

Individuals

Avery, Benjamin Parke (1828-1875), New York journalist, emigrated to California and became part owner of the Marysville Appeal in the 1850s and later published a newspaper in San Francisco and served as state printer. *Californian, pictures in prose and verse* (1878) contains his "word-sketches, " which are largely confined to California scenery, although some picture Native Americans and miners whom he knew when he prospected on the Trinity River in 1850 as well as the city of San Francisco. Most of the book is devoted to poems and essays dealing with mountains of the Coast Range, the Sierra Nevadas, and the Santa Cruz range and their passes and lakes; Yosemite, upper Sacramento Valley, Mount Shasta, and the geysers.

Bidwell, John, (1819-1900) was born in Chautauqua County, New York, and was living in Ohio when he decided to seek his fortune in California in 1841. He journeyed west as part of the first emigrant train going overland from Missouri to California, where he found work at Fort Sutter. He sided with governor Micheltorena in the 1844 revolt but aided the Bear Flag rebels in 1846. After serving with Frémont, he returned to Fort Sutter. Among the first to find gold on Feather River, Bidwell used his earnings to secure a grant north of Sacramento in 1849, and he spent the rest of his life as a farmer at "Rancho Chico, " becoming a leader of the State's agricultural interests. A Democrat and Unionist during the Civil War, Bidwell served in the U.S. House, 1864-66, and was the Prohibition Party's candidate for governor (1890) and President (1892). Throughout his life in California, he was a friend to Native American tribes. John Steele (1832-1915) traveled overland from Wisconsin to California in 1850 and remained for three years. Returning east, he taught school, served in the Union Army, and became an Episcopal minister after the Civil War. *Echoes of the past about California* and *In Camp and Cabin* (1928) reprints works by Bidwell and Steele published earlier. Bidwell's narrative was composed in 1889 and first published in 1890 in the Century Magazine. The version used as a source here as "*Echoes of the past,* " however, was based on a somewhat different version published in pamphlet form by the Chico, California *Advertiser* after Bidwell's death in 1900. This version does not include Bidwell's "*Journey to California,* " the journal that he kept in 1841 and which was published in Missouri in 1843 or 1844 (and appears as part of his Addresses, reminiscences..., 1906). The memoir focuses on Bidwell's overland journey to California, with some attention to his early years in the West: acquaintance with Johann Sutter, and early gold discoveries. Steele's *In Camp and Cabin*, first published in 1901, recounts Steele's experiences mining in camps near Nevada City and the American River, with tales of trips to Feather River, Los Angeles, and an expedition to San Andres and camps on the Mokelumne, Calaveras, and Stanislaus Rivers. He provides numerous anecdotes of the people of the camps and their varied national and ethnic backgrounds with many tales of crime and lawlessness. He also discusses contrasting mining methods and gives special attention to Hispanic and Native American Californians whom he met.

Brewer, William Henry (1828-1910) was a professor of chemistry at Washington College in Pennsylvania when he joined the staff of California's first State Geologist, Josiah Dwight Whitney, 1860-1864. On returning east, Brewer became Professor of Agriculture at Yale, a post he held for nearly forty years. Up and down California (1930) collects Brewer's letters and journal entries recording his work with Whitney's geological survey of California, chronicling not merely the survey's scientific work but also the social, agricultural, and economic life of the state from south to north as the survey's men passed along. New Haven, Yale university press; London, H. Milford, Oxford university press, 1930.

CLEMENS, SAMUEL LANGHORNE (1835-1910), better known as "Mark Twain, " left Missouri in 1861 to work with his brother, the newly appointed Secretary of the Nevada Territory. Once settled in Nevada, Clemens fell victim to gold fever and went to the Humboldt mines. When prospecting lost its attractions, Clemens found work as a reporter in Virginia City. In 1864, Clemens moved to California and worked as a reporter in San Francisco. It was there that he began to establish a nationwide reputation as a humorist. Roughing it (1891), first published in 1872, is his account of his adventures in the Far West. He devotes twenty chapters to the overland journey by boat and stagecoach to Carson City, including several chapters on the Mormons. Next come chronicles of mining life and local politics and crime in Virginia City and San Francisco and even a junket to the Hawaiian Islands. The book closes with his return to San Francisco and his introduction to the lecture circuit.

FAIRCHILD, LUCIUS (1831-1896) left Madison, Wisconsin, for California in 1849 and remained in the West until 1858. On his return to Wisconsin, Fairchild carved out a remarkable career as a soldier-politician: serving in a Wisconsin regiment in the Civil War, winning election as governor in 1866, and then representing the United States abroad in a variety of diplomatic posts. California letters of Lucius Fairchild (1931) records his overland journey to California, gold prospecting from Calaveras County to Scott Valley, business partnership with Elijah Steele in farming, mining, and butchering in Scott Valley.

HOUGHTON, ELIZA DONNER, (b. 1843) was the youngest child of George Donner, one of two Springfield, Illinois, brothers who organized the ill-fated California-bound emigrant party that bore their name. Eliza and her older sisters were rescued by relief parties that made their way to the stranded travellers at Donner Lake, but their parents perished, and the girls were left to make their way alone in the West. The expedition of the Donner party and its tragic fate (1911) begins with Mrs. Houghton's account of her childhood and the family's tragic overland journey, and rescue. She continues with her life as an orphan, first at Fort Sutter, and then with a family in Sonoma and with her older half-sister in Sacramento. She describes the impact of the Gold Rush and new immigration on the area, farm work and domestic work and her own education in public schools and St. Catherine's Convent in Benicia. She writes at length of the emotional scars caused by contemporary rumors of cannibalism among the Donner Party and offers full accounts of Donner family history as well as the background of her husband, Samuel Houghton. An appen-dix contains several documentary sources for the history of the Donner Party. Chicago, A.C. McClurg & co., 1911 [Mrs. Houghton writes in her preface: *"Who better than survivors knew the heart-rending circumstances of life and death in those mountain camps? Yet who can wonder that tenderest recollections and keenest heartaches silenced their quivering lips for many years; and left opportunities for false and sensational details to be spread by morbid collectors of food for excitable brains, and for prolific historians who too readily accepted exaggerated and un-authentic versions as true statements? I then resolved that, "When I grow to be a woman I shall tell the story of my party so clearly that no one can doubt its truth"? Who can doubt that my resolve has been ever kept fresh in mind, by eager research for verification and by diligent communica-tion with older survivors, and rescuers sent to our relief, who answered my many questions and cleared my obscure points? "* Use your own judgement of the voracity of infor-mation provided in newspaper accounts of the time.

HUNTLEY, SIR HENRY VERE (1795-1864) was a Brit-ish naval officer and colonial administrator. *California: its gold and its inhabitants* (1856) contains his experiences in California in 1852 as the San Francisco-based representa-tive of a British gold quartz-mining company. He describes business and social life in San Francisco as well as visits to Marysville and Sacramento and two months at Placerville supervising large-scale mechanized mining operations. Special attention is given to shipping news, crime and violence and political corruption and disasters such as the Marysville flood and Sacramento fire.

KIP, RIGHT REV. WILLIAM INGRAHAM (1811-1893) left New York in December 1853 to become Missionary Bishop and later the first Diocesan Bishop of the Protestant Episcopal Church for California. The early days of his episcopate (1892) contains reminiscences of his rectorship of Grace Church, San Francisco; visits to Sacramento, Stockton, San José, Monterey, Benicia, and Los Angeles; experiences in mining camps in Marysville, Grass Val-ley, and Nevada; and the history of church politics and rivalries.

MASSEY, ERNEST DE, was the younger son of a well-to-do French family who sailed to America for the Gold Rush in the spring of 1849. He eventually settled in San Fran-cisco where he lived until his return to Europe in 1857. A Frenchman in the Gold Rush (1927) is a translation of de Massey's journal covering his voyage to California, gold mining on the Trinity River in 1850, and visits to San José, Santa Cruz, and San Juan Bautista; and his career as a San Francisco businessman and journalist, 1850-1851.

McILHANY, EDWARD WASHINGTON (b. 1828) left West Virginia for the California gold fields in 1849. Recollections of a 49er (1908) describes his overland journey west, gold prospecting on Feather River and Grass Valley, hunting and trapping, proprietorship of a general store and hotel in Onion Valley, the Colorado gold rush, and Missouri railroading after the Civil War.

MEYER, CARL, OF BASEL was a German-speaking Swiss who traveled to California in 1849. Bound for Sacramento (1938) is the English translation of Nach dem Sacramento, published in the Swiss town of Aarau in 1855. Meyer begins with his 1849 voyage from New Orleans, continuing with tales of the Mariposa and Trinidad gold mines, Stockton, San Francisco, Sacramento, and Mormon Island. Claremont, Calif., Saunders studio press, 1938

MUIR, JOHN (1838-1914), famed naturalist, came to Wisconsin as a boy and studied at the University of Wisconsin. He first came to California in 1868 and devoted six years to the study of the Yosemite Valley. After work in Nevada, Utah, and Colorado, he returned to California in 1880 and made the state his home. One of the heroes of America's conservation movement, Muir deserves much of the credit for making the Yosemite Valley a protected national park and for alerting Americans to the need to protect this and other natural wonders. "The mountains of California" (1894) is his book length tribute to the beauties of the Sierras. He recounts not only his own journeys by foot through the mountains, glaciers, forests, and valleys, but also the geological and natural history of the region, ranging from the history of glaciers, the patterns of tree growth, and the daily life of animals and insects. While Yosemite naturally receives great attention, Muir also expounds on less well known beauty spots. New York, The Century Company1894.

PETERS, CHARLES, born in Portugal in 1825, first visited California in 1846 as a merchant seaman, returning three years later to seek gold at Columbia, Jackson Creek, and Mokelumne Hill. "The Autobiography of Charles Peters" (1915) is the old man's brief memoir of his life through the 1850s, followed by a series of "Good Luck" stories, miscellaneous tales of the mining camps, a few of which seem to be credited to Peters although most are the work of another author, drawn from many sources.

RICE, HARVEY (1800-1891), a Cleveland lawyer and newspaper publisher, and his wife traveled by rail to California in 1869. Letters from the Pacific slope (1870) contains Rice's account of that journey, broken by side trips to Salt Lake City, Carson City, and Lake Tahoe. Spending nearly a month in and near San Francisco, the Rices sail south to San Pedro and Los Angeles with a stop at Santa Barbara. They visit ranches, vineyards, and orchards in the neighborhood. Note that his quote on page 151 seems exaggerated or erroneous. He notes "wagons carrying thirty to sixty tons" which is more than a modern 18 wheeler carries. It's more likely that it was three to six tons.

RYAN, WILLIAM REDMOND (1791-1855), an Englishman, enlisted in an American regiment bound for California and sailed round the Horn in 1847. Personal adventures in Upper and Lower California (1850), chronicles his daily life at the Stanislaus Mine; his career as a trader; travels through Stockton, Monterey, and Sacramento; life in San Francisco, 1849; the Constitutional Convention; and return voyage via Panama, 1849.

SCHAEFFER, LUTHER MELANCHTHON. A native of Frederick, Maryland, Luther Melanchthon Schaeffer sailed around the Horn to California in 1849. He spent most of the next two-and-a-half years in the gold fields, mining on the Feather River, Deer Creek, Grass Valley (Centerville) and other Nevada County sites. Sketches of travels in South America, Mexico and California (1860) gives an excellent picture of the international, interracial community of miners with comments on social patterns, creation of local government, vigilance committees, and legal disputes in this society. Schaeffer also describes visits to San Francisco and Sacramento, Mexico, and Panama before his return to the East in 1852. New-York, J. Egbert, printer, 1860.

SHERMAN, WILLIAM TECUMSEH (1820-1891) of Ohio won military fame as one of the greatest Union generals in the Civil War. His association with California began when he served as an aide to Generals Philip Kearny and Richard Barnes Mason during the Mexican War. He remained in California as an adjutant to General Persifer Smith. Sherman's military tour in California ended in January 1850, but he resigned his Army commission in 1853 and returned to California as manager of a new bank. Barring a brief trip east to bring his wife and daughter to their new home in San Francisco, Sherman remained until 1857. "Recollections of California" (1945) contains extracts from Sherman's published memoirs dealing with his life in California as well as two letters written by Sherman from Monterey in 1848. These cover his voyage round the Horn and landing in Monterey and military missions to Los Angeles and San Francisco. He discusses the Army's problems of establishing military rule and recalls the discovery of gold, which transformed the military mission and his own life. Sherman chronicles his part in Governor Mason's historic inspection trip to the gold fields near Sutter's Fort in 1848 as well as his own business ventures of the time: a store at Coloma, surveying a channel through Suisuin Bay, a ranch at Cosumnes River and Sacramento land speculations. He describes San Francisco and the flood of immigrants to California, 1848-1849. From his later residence, he recalls the bank run of 1855 and the Vigilance Committee crisis of 1856. The excerpts end with Sherman's recollections of his life as attorney and educator, 1857-1861 before the Civil War called him back to military life.

UPHAM, SAMUEL CURTIS (1819-1885) was a clerk in a Philadelphia merchant house when he decided to try his luck in California in January 1849. Sailing round the Horn, he visited Rio de Janeiro and Talcahuana before landing in San Francisco. After a brief career as a gold miner at the Calaveras diggings, Upham moved to Sacramento, where he published the Sacramento Transcript, May-August 1850. Notes of a voyage to California (1878) includes Upham's memoirs of his early years in California, with special attention to Sacramento's colorful history in 1850. He closes his narrative with a brief description of his return to Philadelphia that same year via Panama. The book's lengthy appendix contains chapters on California journalism, the California exhibition at the 1876 Centennial Exhibition, and various reunion dinners and other events sponsored by the California "Pioneers" Association.

WHITE, WILLIAM FRANCIS (1829-1891?) and his young wife sailed from New York in 1849 round the Horn to San Francisco, where he set up an import business. He later represented Santa Cruz in the state constitutional convention and served as a bank commissioner. A picture of pioneer times in California (1881), written under the pseudonym "William Grey, " presents White's revisionist version of California history challenging the picture presented in the 1854 Annals of San Francisco. In particular, he attacks the Annals' discussion of the Mission Fathers and the Mission Indians, the United States conquest of California in the Mexican War, discovery of gold at Sutter's Fort, and the role of women during the Gold Rush. He also reminisces about his voyage to California and experiences as a San Francisco merchant, 1849-1850, as well as legends of the gold mines. The volume concludes with three fictional tales of California in the Gold Rush.

Index

Photo Index

More Golden Corridor Books

The Golden Corridor is an overview of the life and times in Northern California in the 19th century. It is distinctive because it brings together the unique observations and viewpoints of dozens of people who were in a particular area at a particular time-frame in history.

The Golden Corridor has paved the way for a more in-depth look at various Northern California communities. You'll find *The Golden Quest* a fun and informative book about Lake Tahoe and the Western Nevada mining districts (the Comstock Lode).

We made some exciting "finds" in our first two books and there is more to discover, preserve and share. Through today's technology, information that could only be obtained looking through huge historical texts in vast research libraries and archives is now accessible to everyone. And we'll bring it to you.

More *Golden Corridor* books are in the works. They will be even more informative and more fun for readers. They will include more photographic treasures and information from the archives of dozens of smaller historical societies and private collections. And, we're working with the community of historians, docents and various historical parks and friends, to discover even more new sources of information.

Over the next couple of years you'll be able to visit many places and see many scenes that few have experienced. Here are some titles and estimated release dates:

The Golden Hub, Sacramento	Spring 2008
The Golden Gate, San Francisco	Spring 2009

To pre-order copies of any of these books, or for bulk orders for schools or other organizations, please contact us at:

19thCentury Books / Electric Canvas
1001 Art Road
Pilot Hill, CA 95664
916.933.4490

If you'd like to receive an e-mail announcement when new titles are released, please contact: Jody@19thCentury.us

Thank you for your interest in our rich history. We hope you've enjoyed *The Golden Corridor* and will enjoy more of our books in the future.

Does your family have 19th century photos, journals, letters or other documents you'd like to share and preserve?

Let us help you archive your originals electronically. You will receive a copy of all your materials on CD, and you decide if you'd like to retain the originals or entrust them to your local historical society, the Library of Congress, or some other institution for safekeeping.

Please share your family's history. It'll provide one more piece to the complex puzzle that represents our rich culture and background.

Please contact us for details.